FEMALE CIRCUMCISION/FEMALE GENITAL MUTILATION: A HUMAN RIGHTS VIOLATION

FEMALE CIRCUMCISION/ FEMALE GENITAL MUTILATION: A HUMAN RIGHTS VIOLATION

A Case Study of Ethiopia

Shiyal, Chandni Ratilal Tarla

GenNext Publication

ISBN : 978-93-8022-244-8

Price: ₹ 540

First Published, 2015

Published by

GenNext Publication
23, Main Ansari Road,
Darya Ganj, New Delhi-110002.
Ph. : 9212142040
E-mail: kalpaz@hotmail.com

Laser Typesetting : Sanya Computers, Delhi
Printed at : G. Print Process, Delhi

Cataloging in Publication Data—DK
Courtesy: D.K. Agencies (P) Ltd. <docinfo@dkagencies.com>

Shiyal, Chandni Ratilal Tarla, author.
Female circumcision/female genital mutilation : a human rights violation : a case study of Ethiopia / Shiyal, Chandni Ratilal Tarla.
pages cm
Includes bibliographical references (pages) and index.
ISBN 9789380222448

1. Female circumcision—Africa. 2. Female circumcision—Ethiopia. 3. Women's rights—Africa. 4. Women's rights—Ethiopia. I. Title.

DDC 618.16059096 23

This book is dedicated to
all the girls, who have been the victims of
female circumcision/female genital mutilation.

I hope this practice can be eradicated in all its forms in the years ahead.

Contents

Preface

While pursuing my M.Phil degree at the Centre for African Studies, I came across the term Female Circumcision/Female Genital Mutilation (FC/FGM) for the first time. Being a feminist ideologist and out of genuine curiosity I commenced research on this topic and became aware of unbelievable facts about this inhuman practice.

I consider FC/FGM a crime not only against women in Africa but against humanity because it violates the rights of women over their sexuality. I also got to know that many people are not aware of this practice. In the course of writing my dissertation on the subject, I studied experiences of victims of this practice and was once again shocked to know that women themselves supported FC/FGM and played a key role in its perpetuation. FC/FGM reflects the entrenched patriarchal values that advocate that FC/FGM is a mark of virginity among women. At the same time I also read about women victims who have turned their suffering into strength and stood up to fight against this evil practice. Former victims are now anti-FGM activists and now save other girls from undergoing trauma due to the performance of FC/FGM.

My main objective for writing this book is to spread the message that African women should educate their daughters and make them vocal to safeguard their own rights and live life on their own terms. There is hope that advances in the level of awareness and the collective efforts against this practice by the international community, regional and local NGOs who have been working selflessly may lead to the eradication of FC/FGM.

I strongly believe that each society has a set of ideas, traditional beliefs and religious practices which have social sanctions, but practices such as FC/FGM consider women as an object and make them subservient to men. This work advocates that under the guise of traditions and religion, women must not subject themselves to FC/FGM as it degrades womanhood under the pretext of cultural relativity. There need to be a universal condemnation against this practice.

This book is a small attempt to share my concern for the women and girls who have been subjected to FC/FGM; in particular my African sisters and I hope my efforts result in a FC/FGM free Africa and the world at large.

Acknowledgements

I would like to extend my deep gratitude and the efforts of my teacher Dr. Renu Modi, who always helped and encouraged me in writing this book. I thank her for reposing trust in me and sparing her valuable time for the completion of this book.

I thank my priest Jai Darshitashriji and Hemanshushriji for their blessing for the completion of this book.

I thank my mom, dad and Hiren Narsey, who have provided all kinds of support for pursuing higher education and fulfil my academic aspirations.

I also express my gratitude to a senior Ethiopian government official, Genet Teshome, who was posted at the Ethiopian Consulate in Mumbai. He provided me with important primary resources for this research. During his visit to the Centre for African Studies, he was very generous and found time to communicate and share his valuable insights on the subject.

I would like to thank for the help offered by Valerie and Ismail Ali Gardo, who work at an NGO, named the Afar Pastoralist Development Association (APDA). They provided me with important information about their NGO, and its activities for the eradication of Female Circumcision/Female Genital Mutilation (FC/FGM).

I am highly grateful for contribution of my friend Ashish, who helped me identifying the subject of my research, earlier on. I thank my best friend Amreen, who always motivated me to write this book. My special thanks to Pranav Jani for cheering me up to write this book. Sarita, Chitra, Sanju, Chandreyi, Gargi, Veenita, S. Maurya and Yashmin always said, "You can do it". Thank you all my dear friends for being with me always and sharing yours ideas during writing this book. I would also like to thank the entire team of Gyan Books for their assistance in shaping this book.

Finally, I wish to dedicate this book to all the girls, who have been subjected to and are at the risk of undergoing the heinous practice of Female Circumcision / Female Genital Mutilation (FC / FGM). I hope this archaic practice must eradicate forever from this world and the young and innocent girls' shouldn't be the victim of this inhuman practice so that they can live with full freedom and choices about how to move ahead with their own existence.

List of Tables

List of Figures

Abbreviations

AI	:	Amnesty International
AIDOS	:	Association for Women in Development
AIDS	:	Acquired Immuno Deficiency Syndrome
APDA	:	Afar Pastoralist Development Association
AU	:	African Union
BCC	:	Behaviour Change Communication
CCA	:	Common Country Assessment
CHA	:	Community Health Agents
CEDAW	:	Committee on the Elimination on the all forms of Discrimination against Women
CMC	:	Community Management Committee
CNAPN	:	National Committee to Fight Harmful Practices
CPA	:	Child Protection Advocate
CPC	:	Child Protection Committee
CRC	:	Convention on the Rights of the Child
CSW	:	Commission on the Status of Women
DHS	:	Demographic and Health Surveys
EDHS	:	Ethiopia Demographic and Health Survey
EGLDAM	:	Ye Ethiopia Goji Limadawi Dirgitoch Aswogaj Maherber
FC/FGM	:	Female Circumcision/Female Genital Mutilation
FGM	:	Female Genital Mutilation
FIGO	:	Federation of International Gynecology and Obstetrics

GAD	:	Gender and Development
GAMCOTRAP	:	Gambian Committee on Traditional Practices
HIV	:	*Human Immunodeficiency Virus*
HRBA	:	Human Rights-Based Approach
HTP	:	Harmful Traditional Practices
IAC	:	Inter-African Committee
ICCPR	:	International Covenant on Civil and Political Rights
ICESCR	:	International Covenant on Economic Social and Cultural Rights
ICJ	:	The International Commission of Jurists
ICPD	:	International Conference on Population and Development
IEC	:	Information Education and Communication
INTACT	:	The International Network to Analyse, Communicate and Transform the Campaign against Female Genital Mutilation/Cutting
KMG	:	Kembatti Mentti Gezzimma
LFA	:	Logical Framework Approach
MDG	:	Millennium Development Goals
M&E	:	Monitoring and Evaluation
MICS	:	Multiple Indicator Cluster Surveys
NCHR	:	National Commission of Human Rights
NCTPE	:	The National Committee on Traditional Practices in Ethiopia
NGO	:	Non-Governmental Organisation
NPWJ	:	No Peace Without Justice
OAU	:	Organisation of African Unity
OBGYN	:	Obstetrics and Gynaecology

PAPFAM	:	Pan Arab Project for Family Health
PAP	:	Pan-African Parliament
PMC	:	Population Media Centre
REACH	:	Reproductive Educative and Community Health
RVF	:	Recto Vaginal Fistula
SARA	:	The Support for Analysis and Research in Africa
SCN-E	:	Save the Children of Norway-Ethiopia
SIDA	:	Swedish International Development Co-operation Agency
SNNPR	:	Southern Nations Nationalities and People's Region
STD	:	Sexually Transmitted Diseases
UDHR	:	United Nations Universal Declaration of Human Rights
UK	:	United Kingdom
UN	:	United Nations
UEMOA	:	West African Economic and Monetary Union
UNDAF	:	UN Development Assistance Framework
UNFPA	:	United Nations Population Fund
UNHCR	:	UN High Commissioner for Refugees
UNICEF	:	United Nations Children's Fund
USA	:	United States of America
VVF	:	Vesico Vaginal Fistula
WEL	:	Women Empowerment Link
WHO	:	World Health Organisation
WID	:	Women in Development

A Poem on Female Circumcision/ Female Genital Mutilation from Somalia

Birth of a baby must be a blessing event,
But mine was nothing short of a curse.
Daddy's face didn't shine. Drums didn't make noise,
No shots were fired. No ceremony was held.
The new born was me. I am a girl,
In my culture, gender counts most.
A girl is not as welcome as a baby boy.
Raising camel in the rangeland
is family's highest priority.
They believe a girl has no hands for that
harsh combat against the enemies
is family's highest priority.
They believe a girl has no heart for that
reconciliation in the aftermath of a clash
is family's highest priority.
They believe a girl has no brain for that
at five I had to face the worst.
A knife cut across my genitals,
A mid-wife circumcised me,
Stitched me. Infibulated me,
where I used to have a clit.
I have a black scar now,
why inflict me with this pain?
This real pain of primitive cultures
in tears I am, at every stage of my life
Mom and Dad, I'm I not a daughter?
Dear Brother, I'm I not a sister?
Dear mankind, wherever you are
I'm, I not a human being?
Tears, Tears, Tears.

By Abdi-Noor H. Mohamed

Source : Women's UN Report Network 2012.

Introduction

The concept gender inequality is still very much prevalent across the world, though the level of this inhuman practices differs from county to country. More specifically in developing countries, gender inequality is much in practice as compared to developed countries. It is due to poverty, illiteracy, entrenched patriarchy and other contributing factors that have kept women subordinate to men even in the present century. Societal pressures and unfounded cultural practices do not allow women to raise their voice against brutal practices imposed on them. The question of women being equal to men is still remains elusive in the form of utopia !

Till date women blame themselves for all the miseries and tortures faced by them in their day to day life. Due to this constricted mentality, male domination and patriarchy still prevails across societies (Leslie 1994: p.79).

According to the World Bank

> *Many violent acts such as rape, female battering, sexual harassment and other harmful practices such as Female Circumcision/Female Genital Mutilation (FC/FGM) are a significant cause for disability among women. These forms of violence cause physical harm, psychological, social, and mental suffering and violate women's and girl's human rights as well* (Rwomire 2001).

This study aims to analyse the manner in which justifications based on historical, ideological, social, cultural; and religious base support heinous and violent social practices against women such as FC/FGM which is the research subject of this book. In academic discourse on FC/FGM, the term "female circumcision", "female genital cutting", "female genital surgery", "ritual genital surgery" and "sexual mutilation", "female genital mutilation" are used interchangeably (Rahman and Toubia 2000: p. 4). However, throughout this book the researcher is using the general term FC/FGM, to describe the subject under study. Patriarchy, gender discrimination and strong religious cultural support are some of the common factors that facilitate the occurrence of FC/FGM that is an entrenched practice in various countries across the African continent.

In 1997, the World Health Organisation (WHO), United Nations Population Fund (UNFPA), United Nations Children's Fund (UNICEF) defined FC/FGM as:

> *The collective name, given to several different traditional practices that involve the cutting of female genitals. It comprises of all procedures involving partial or total removal of the external female genitalia or other injury to the female genital organs for non-medical reasons* (WHO 2008: p. 4).

While in the same year, these three organisations issued a joint statement on FC/FGM which described "the implication of the practice for public health and human rights, and declared support for its abandonment" (WHO 2008: p. 3).

Human rights are "'universal moral rights'. They are universal in that they are the rights that people possess by virtue of being human beings, regardless of race, sex, nationality, occupation, income, religion, and other social and cultural characteristics". The question that is pertinent is, are women's rights human rights? Women's rights will be seen as human rights only if women are considered as complete human beings, and their rights are understood as equal to men (Rwomire 2001: pp. 68-70).

More than thousands of innocent girls are still unaware of the practice of FC/FGM to be practiced on them as part of their culture. The prevalence of FC/FGM is 29 countries in Africa and the Middle East, where the practice is concentrated, more than 125 million girls and women have been cut. Whereas according to UNFPA report, 86 million young girls world-wide are predicted to undergo some form of FC/FGM by 2030, if there is slow reduction towards its abandonment (UNFPA 2014).

The practice of FC/FGM is unfortunately and ironically, inflicted by women on women though it has its roots in patriarchy. It also concentrates on how African women themselves play a key role in continuation of this evil practice and pass on this practice as a cultural trait to their next generation of women. FC/FGM is considered a mark of celibacy for young African girls; therefore, mothers inflict this practice on their daughters, as a pre-requisite for a good marital life. But in reality, FC/FGM is a factor significantly responsible for the severe physical, mental and health complications.

FC/FGM is usually performed on girls between the age of four and twelve as a rite of passage of womanhood. The time at which the practice is performed varies in different cultures. In some cultures, it is performed soon after a girl is born or it is performed just before marriage or after first pregnancy. FC/FGM is performed on girls by traditional practitioners or by an older woman within the family (Rahman and Toubia 2000: p. 3).

Earlier the practice of FC/FGM was thought to have an impact only on health and mental well-being. But cutting of healthy genital organs for non-medical reasons without the consent of girl is a basic violation of girls and women's right and has serious and hazardous repercussions on the reproductive health of a girl. It is shocking that FC/FGM is performed at very young and impressionable ages between four and twelve years, when the girl is so innocent and is not aware about the consequences of this heartless practice (*ibid*).

FC/FGM contravenes human rights of children as protected by the Convention on the Rights of the Child (CRC). The issue of FC/FGM is now increasingly discussed within the framework of girl's and women's rights rather than just as a health or medical issue (*ibid*).

There have been sustained efforts by various world

organisations namely; the WHO, the UNFPA and the UNICEF to generate social awareness against FC/FGM. New ways have now systematically institutionalised FC/FGM, through the concepts such as "medicalisation" of FC/FGM. This has resulted in higher prevalence of FC/FGM by reducing the health risks involved in the process as more advanced and sophisticated ways of cutting are now adopted. Various world organisations are working towards the abandonment of FC/FGM and ban the process of "medicalisation" of FC/FGM. They are discouraging medical practitioners who are practicing "medicalisation" of FC/FGM for generating money (WHO 2010: pp. 8-10).

Though FC/FGM occurs in several African countries, this book attempts a micro-study of Ethiopia, the focus of this research work. Women's status in terms of social, economic and health is unequal as compared to men in Ethiopia. This is yet another indicator of the fact that patriarchy is strongly rooted in Ethiopian society as in other countries of Africa (UNFPA and Population Council 2010: p.1). The Ethiopian case has been used as a representative case study to understand the low socio-economic and cultural status of women as well as the violation of their sexuality in the form of rape, abduction FC/FGM, etc. in Ethiopia (Ethiopian Society of Population Studies 2008: p. 18) and holds true for other parts of the continent as well.

In the Afar region of Ethiopia, 90 per cent of girls are mutilated due to their culture and tradition (UNFPA and Population Council 2010). Till now, 23.8 million girls have undergone FC/FGM in Ethiopia which stands second after Egypt where 27.2 million girls are mutilated, this figure itself show the seriousness of the problem faced by millions of girls (UNICEF 2013: p. 2).

There is a growing concerns regarding violence against women. Interventions at the national, international level; through policies, media, NGOs, art, culture, religious discourses are being used as a medium to highlight the entrenched malpractices such as FC/FGM and raise awareness and combat violence against women. In 2012, in Sweden, one such attempt was made through the use of art. The Swedish Cultural Minister Lena Adelsohn Liljeroth was invited to speak at World Art Day about the freedom of art and asked to cut a cake shaped in the form of a naked black woman to highlight and raise awareness about the issue of FC/FGM. The motive behind this incident was of social awareness about FC/FGM but due to unconventional mode of representation, it became controversial and resulted in a negative and violent response all over the world. It was seen as being culturally insensitive (BBC News, 18 April 2012).

The artist who conceptualised the idea of cake in the form of a naked black woman was Makode Linde. Linde is a black artist, who was born and raised in Stockholm. He says his work has been misunderstood and explained that "his art had tackled different prejudices and ideas of oppression for many years. Further, he added that I've been doing this by revamping black faces into different contexts, so when the Swedish Art Organisation asked me to design a cake for them it felt totally natural". The TT news agency reported that Ms Liljeroth had said she could "understand that this can feel provocative..." (*ibid*).

Several attempts have been made to raise awareness about the pertinent subject of gender equity, human rights of women and FC/FGM. In 2012, 'African Voices' interviewed three Diaspora-based women on the international news channel CNN.

Rainatou Sow, one of the interviewees and the founder and executive director of an organisation "Make Every Woman Count" was also named as "Inspirational Woman of 2012" by the UK (United Kingdom) group "Women for Africa". She stated that by using social media, especially internet as a medium, her organisation is trying to reach out to every African women and give them a platform to express their voices that they are worthy of respect as human beings (CNN News, 30 November 2012).

Marie-Claire Faray, an activist from the Democratic Republic of Congo and a member of the Women's

International League for Peace and Freedom has been working relentlessly to end violence against women in her home country. Through her efforts, she hopes to bring women on board and attempts to bring changes at individual, local, national and international level. She is a steadfast believer in Gandhi's views that "If you want to see change, you start it within yourself" and she is definitely a role model as an activist on issues of women's human rights (*ibid*).

Yet, another African women Betty Makoni, a Zimbabwean activist continues her struggle to rescue girls from sexual abuse in her own country in particular and Africa in general. The traumatic circumstances of being a victim of sexual abuse at a tender age of six and having lost her mother at the age of nine had a deep impact on her. These led her to devote her life to protect other young women and girls from abuse. Through her programme named "Girl Child Network" she is protecting more than 300,000 girls in Zimbabwe from sexual abuse. She was also named as a CNN Hero in the year 2009. In her interview with CNN she said, "life experiences of Africans have been very complicated since past centuries. History did not want to go against religions and harmful cultural practices... but since the past decade, the new generation does not consider themselves as victims. According to Ms Makoni, there is a need to work on the ground rather than using sophisticated logical framework. There is a need for inspiration and a platform where women themselves can advocate their concerns and anti-FC/FGM views for themselves and turn into an ideal society and be the change they wish to see" (*ibid*).

Thus, we see that various gender activists concerned with issues of women are against practices of gender violence including FC/FGM. They actively support and advocate solutions from within the continent to these issues from a human rights perspective.

The US Secretary of State Hillary Clinton's remarks on FC/FGM were as follows:

> *We cannot excuse this as a cultural tradition. There are many cultural traditions that used to exist in many parts*

> *of the world that are no longer acceptable. We cannot excuse it as a private matter because it has very broad public implications. It has no medical benefits. It is plain and simple a human rights violation* (UNFPA 2012 b).

Ambassador Hillary Clinton made her position very clear, wherein she advocated respect for cultural differences, but at the same time she did not support the practice of FC/FGM, which is unacceptable on grounds of human rights violation (*ibid*).

Babatunde Osotimehin, a Nigerian medico and Nigeria's former health minister, the executive director of the UNFPA since 2011 as well as the UN's under-secretary general asserted, "Women are not just women, but human beings". His main aim is to achieve gender equality, reduce poverty and help hundreds of millions in developing countries. During the CNN interview, he talked about his mother, who was an entrepreneur and donned various roles of a mother, wife, community leader and believer of social justice. For him his mother has been a role model and his socialisation took place in a way where equality between men and women was taught. Osotimehin says, it is necessary to change the status of women all over the world. According to Osotimehin,

> *Beyond just legislation or policies, we need to confront these issues to make a difference... all his life he will continue working for rights of women and believes women will change the world. [As a teacher in a medical school, my best students were women. As physicians they are the best and, really, when you look at different aspects of life, even peace-building, women they build better peace. So, let's give them a chance* (CNN News, 20th November 2012).

During his entire career Osotimehin has worked in a dedicated manner for the development and human rights of women.

However, this issue has not received adequate attention by African leadership and policy-makers. Therefore, national as well as international organisations such as UNFPA,

UNICEF, WHO and other organisations have put in place several programmes for the awareness and preventive measures to abandon this practice. As a part of its advocacy programme, the International Day of Zero Tolerance to FC/FGM is observed each year to raise awareness about this practice on 6th February (WHO 2012). Therefore, it is necessary to eradicate this evil social practice on moral grounds, because it is a discriminatory and cruel practice.

This book is divided into four chapters: The first chapter, *Understanding Female Circumcision/Female Genital Mutilation in Africa* traces the history behind the practice of FC/FGM and locates the theoretical framework of the problem. In the second chapter, *Female Circumcision/Female Genital Mutilation: A Case Study of Ethiopia*, the overall scenario of FC/FGM in Ethiopia is examined and reasons behind the continuation of this practice as well as positive signs of changing patterns in the prevalence of the practice through role of NGOs and international organisations. The third chapter, *Female Circumcision/Female Genital Mutilation: National Response from Human Rights Perspective in Africa*, emphasises on a human rights-based approach (HRBA) and how FC/FGM is a violation of these rights and discusses the role of national and international organisations to eradicate FC/FGM in Africa in general and Ethiopia in particular. The fourth chapter, *The Role of International Organisations to Eradicate Female Circumcision/Female Genital Mutilation in Africa* discusses the role of the international organisations namely; the WHO, the UNFPA and the UNICEF, and others for protecting women and girls who are forced to undergo this practice because of the unequal social structures through their Joint Programmes. Finally, it concludes with the main findings of chapters and future prospects for the improvement of the status of women and girls in the coming years towards the practice of FC/FGM.

References

BBC News (18th April 2012). 'Swedish Minister in 'Racist Cake' Controversy' [Online], Available at: <http://www.bbc.com/news/world-europe-17749533> (Accessed on 7/6/2012).

CNN (20th November 2012). Reporter Isha Sesay 'UN Director: 'Women will Change the World', [Online], Available at:<http://edition.cnn.com/2012/11/20/world/africa/babatunde-osotimehin-unfpa-women/index.html>(Accessed on 6/1/2013).

CNN (30th November 2012). Reporter Nima Elbagir 'Give African Women a Voice, Say Activists', [Online], Available at: <http://edition.cnn.com/2012/11/30/world/africa/africa-womens-decade-rights/index.html?iid=article_sidebar> (Accessed on 6/1/2013).

Ethiopian Society of Population Studies (2008). *Gender Inequality and Women's Empowerment: In-depth Analysis of the Ethiopian Demographic and Health Survey 2005,* Addis Ababa: UNFPA [Online], Available at:<http://ethiopia.unfpa.org/drive/Gender.pdf> (Accessed on 17/5/ 2012).

Leslie, M.O. (1994). *Recreating Ourselves: African Women and Critical Transformations,* New Jersey: Africa World Press Inc.

Rahman, A. and Toubia, N. (2000). *Female Genital Mutilation: A Guide to Laws and Policies Worldwide,* London: Zed Books [Online], Available at: <http://books.google.co.in/books?hl=en&lr=&id=kEG6GaudxQEC&oi=fnd&pg=PR8&dq=history+of+female+genital+mutilation&ots=e74EjotccQ&sig=UD32rEFAdxnY6oWfu_UFqQVKGQ4#v=onepage&q=history%20of%20female%20genital%20mutilation&f=fals>(Accessed on 19/6/2012).

Rwomire, A. (2001). *African Women and Children: Crisis and Response,* London: Praeger Publication.

UNFPA and Population Council (2010). *Ethiopia Young Adult Survey: A Study in Seven Regions,* New York: UNFPA [Online], Available at: <http://ethiopia.unfpa.org/drive/EthiopianYoungAdultSurvey2010.pdf> (Accessed on 12/6/ 2012).

UNFPA (2012b). *Cultural Tradition' is No Excuse for Female Genital Mutilation/Cutting,* UNFPA [Online], Available at:<https://www.unfpa.org/public/home/news/pid/10080>(Accessed on 11/9/ 2012).

UNFPA (2014). *International Day of Zero Tolerance for Female Genital Mutilation: Statement of Dr. Babatunde Osotimehin, Executive Director, UNFPA, the United Nations Population Fund,* UNFPA [Online], Available at: <http://www.unfpa.org/public/home/news/pid/16602> (Accessed on 10/2/ 2014).

UNICEF (2013). *Female Genital Mutilation/Cutting: A Statistical Overview and Exploration of the Dynamics of Change*, New York: UNICEF [Online], Available at: <http://www.childinfo.org/files/FGMC_Low_Sept2013.pdf> (Accessed on 18/10/ 2013).

WHO (2008). *Eliminating Female Genital Mutilation: An Interagency Statement OHCHR, UNAIDS, UNDP, UNECA, UNESCO, UNFPA, UNHCR, UNICEF, UNIFEM, WHO*, Switzerland: WHO [Online], Available at:<http://www.unfpa.org/webdav/site/global/shared/documents/publications/2008/eliminating_fgm.pdf> (Accessed on 14/7/ 2012).

WHO (2010). *Global Strategy to Stop Health-care Providers from Performing Female Genital Mutilation UNAIDS, UNDP, UNFPA, UNHCR, UNICEF, UNIFEM, WHO, FIGO, ICN, IOM, MWIA, WCPT, WMA*, Switzerland: WHO [Online], Available at: <http://whqlibdoc.who.int/hq/2010/WHO_RHR_10.9_eng.pdf> (Accessed on 31/12/ 2012).

WHO (2012). *International Day of Zero Tolerance to Female Genital Mutilation*, WHO [Online], Available at: <http://www.who.int/mediacentre/events/annual/femalegenitalmutilation/en/index.htl> (Accessed on 15/9/2012).

1 Understanding Female Circumcision/Female Genital Mutilation in Africa

Female Circumcision/Female Genital Mutilation (FC/FGM) has thrived under the guise of entrenched social norm within several communities in Africa. There are variations in the level of prevalence of FC/FGM globally as well as in various countries of Africa. The most recent trend in FC/FGM is the "medicalisation" of this age-old tradition which, in fact, furthers this practice rather than eliminating it. Statistical data in this chapter highlights the prevalence of FC/FGM in various countries among women in the age group of 15-49 years. It also deals with the various causes of FC/FGM namely; social, religious, economic and cultural factors amongst others. Finally, this study focuses on the harmful consequences of FC/FGM on the reproductive health of a girl, and women and analyses the practice within the framework of a serious human right violation. Further, it indicates the relationship between mother's education and prevalence of FC/FGM among their daughters.

Types of FC/FGM

There are four types of FC/FGM are in practice among communities in Africa. These are:

> ***Type 1:*** *Excision of the prepuce, with or without excision of part of or the entire clitoris;*
>
> ***Type 2:*** *Excision of the clitoris with partial or total excision of the labia minora;*
>
> ***Type 3:*** *Excision of part or all of the external genitalia and the stitching/narrowing of the vaginal opening (infibulations); and*

Type 4: *Unclassified: all other operations on the female genitalia,*

That include:

- *The pricking, piercing, stretching or incisions of the clitoris and/ or labia;*
- *Cauterisation by burning the clitoris and surrounding tissue;*
- *Incision to the vaginal wall; scraping (angurya cuts) or cutting of the vagina and surrounding tissue (gishiri cuts); and*
- *Introduction of corrosive substances or herbs into the vagina to cause bleeding or to tighten or narrow it; and any other procedures that falls under the definition of FC/ FGM given above.*

Of these, the most severe form is infibulations (UNFPA 2007: p. 3).

In twenty-eight countries in Africa, and in a few countries in Asia and the Middle East, Types I, II and III FC/FGM have a higher level of occurrence. It is reported that some forms of FC/FGM is also practiced among certain ethnic groups in Central and South America. Women settled in countries outside of their native countries due to migration have undergone FC/FGM or might be at risk or victim of this practice (WHO 2012).

Like female circumcision, male circumcision is yet another evil social practice that is a serious violation of a child's rights. But both the practices are dissimilar from each other. "Male circumcision is the cutting off of the foreskin from the tip of the penis without damaging the organ itself." Unlike male circumcision female circumcision is more dangerous practice which has a serious impact on the health of women and girls. "Male circumcision affirms manhood with its superior social status and associations to virility. Female circumcision is explicitly intended to show a woman her confined role in society and restrain her sexual desires." Both the practices confine clear cut gender discrimination

(Rahman and Toubia 2000: pp. 4-5). The practice of FC/FGM is also undertaken to confirm to the prevalent social norms.

Understanding the Concept of Social Norm in the Context of FC/FGM

"Social norms, unlike social customs, ways, and traditions which are purely descriptive terms used to refer to what most people do and think. Social norms, in addition to encompassing this type of descriptive information, include information of a prescriptive nature, for, beneath the surface, the word norm insinuates that whatever is prevalent is somehow worthy (valued), is a reflection of social values, and is what one should do as a member of the concerned social body". In short, the concept of social norm always has a prescriptive aspect. It is thought that whoever does not follow that the majority of the people are considered as strange, a deviant or misfit. Durkheim in his work entitled "The Rules of Sociological Method" argues "it is possible to gain exhaustive knowledge of the 'social constraints' of a society through a purely study of customs, which allow one to state what majority of the people do" (Dubois 2003: pp. 1-2).

The practice of FC/FGM operates as a self-enforcing social convention or social norm. The communities that follow FC/FGM, it is considered as a socially upheld behavioural rule. Families and individuals, who practice it think that their community expects them to do so. Moreover, they also feel that if they do not follow this practice they will not be considered as a part of the community. In fact, it is necessary for a girl to undergo this practice to become women and be accepted along with the rest of the family as well as by the social group which they belong to (WHO 2010: p. 3).

Various Terms Used for the Practice of FC/FGM

There are different local terms used in various countries with regard to the practice of FC/FGM. Some of the terms used are "*tabara*" in Egypt, "*tabur*" in Sudan and "*bolokoli*" in Mali. These terms are similar to the words "purify" and "cleaning" by the practice of FC/FGM. Similarly, local terms are used for the types of FC/FGM. But these terms vary in different countries. In Sudan, clitoriodectomy is referred to as *sunna,* and infibulations is referred to as *pharaonic.* Likewise, in French speaking Africa, FC/FGM is commonly referred to as excision; while in English-speaking Africa, the term "circumcision" is generally used (Rahman and Toubia 2000: pp. 3-4).

Since many years, the term "female circumcision" has been used to describe the practice of FC/FGM by the international community. Other terms such as "female genital cutting", "female genital surgery", "ritual genital surgery" and "sexual mutilation", have also been used. But since the past decades, the term "female genital mutilation" has been mostly used by women's health and human rights activists because this term sharply explains the seriousness and harmful effects caused by the practice of FC/FGM (*ibid*: p. 4).

There are various organisations who have adopted the term "Female Genital Mutilation (FGM)" which are as follows:

- The World Health Organisation (WHO).
- In 1990, Inter-African Committee ((IAC) also adopted this term at a meeting on Traditional Practices Affecting the Health of Women and Children in Addis Ababa, Ethiopia.
- The international community also used this term in United Nations (UN) conference documents, including those relating to 1994 International Conference on Population and Development (ICPD) in Cairo (Cairo Conference).
- The 1995, World Summit for Social Development in Copenhagen (Copenhagen Summit), and
- The 1995, Fourth World Conference on Women in Beijing (Beijing Conference) (*ibid*).

The term FGM has been widely used by organisations while communicating with communities. As at times, the term FC/FGM leads to scary impact on women. Due to this, certain organisations use local as well as synonymous terms like "female circumcision" or "female genital cutting" while working with communities to make them understand the seriousness of the problem *(ibid)*.

The Origins of FC/FGM

The Historical Context

The practice of "ritual genital surgery" on women is not a known concept. But the practice of FC/FGM is about 2000 years old. Herodotus (oldest Greek historian) states that the practice of FC/FGM was practiced by the Phoenicians, Hittites and Ethiopians, as well as the Egyptians. It is also noted by some scholars that it was practiced in Ancient Egypt, as a sign of distinction among aristocracy, and noticed that type-III FC/FGM, i.e., infibulations was found on Egyptian Mummies (Momoh 2005: p. 5).

Women's virginity is and still continues to be an important factor in Africa as well as Arab nations till date. The most severe type of FC/FGM; infibulation is still being practice in some countries. Greek physicians who visited Egypt said that the practice of FC/FGM was practiced to reduce the sexual pleasure of women. Most of them believe that the practice of FC/FGM was undertaken to get control over women's sexual behaviour. "The Romans performed a technique involving slipping of rings through the labia majora of female slaves to prevent them becoming pregnant and the Scoptsi sect in Russia performed FC/FGM to ensure virginity" (*ibid*).

Historically, FC/FGM has prevailed in almost all known civilisations. It is not labelled in any individual culture or religion. Patriarchy is the root cause for the continuation of FC/FGM. Though this practice has disappeared in the developed world, it continues to prevail in some developing countries, mostly in Africa (*ibid*).

It is found that in 19th century in UK (United Kingdom) and USA (United States of America), the practice of FC/FGM was performed by gynaecologists to cure female weaknesses like nymphomania, insanity, masturbation and other 'female disorders' which now exceeds all religious, racial and social boundaries *(ibid)*.

These attribute the origins of the practice to:

- Ancient Egypt,
- The slave trade when black slave women entered ancient Arab societies,
- The arrival of Islam in some parts of sub-Saharan Africa,
- Sub-Saharan Africa, prior to the arrival of Islam, notably among warrior-like peoples, and
- Ethnic groups in sub-Saharan Africa as part of puberty rites (WHO 2001: p. 37).

Prevalence

There have been enormous efforts at global level to eradicate FC/FGM; still it is highly practiced in a developing world. Statistics states that practice of FC/FGM is performed on three million women and girls every year, and till date about 100 to 140 million have been victims of this practice (UNFPA 2007: p. 1).

The Global Scenario

Most of the women and girls who are at risk of undergoing FC/FGM reside in 29 countries in Africa and Middle East (UNICEF 2013: p. 22). FC/FGM has also been found to be practiced within certain populations in India, Indonesia and Malaysia. In the Arab States, it is mostly practiced among some communities on the Red Sea coast of Yemen. It is also reported that FC/FGM is practiced among other parts of the world, such as in Europe and North America, where some immigrant families from countries that practice FC/FGM have now settled (UNFPA 2007: pp. 1-2).

In Asia, the practice of FC/FGM is found to be practiced by Daudi Bohra Muslims in India and a few Muslim ethnic groups in Sri Lanka (Rahman and Toubia 2000: p. 7). There is no confirmed evidence, though some data states that few cases of FC/FGM are being practised in Jordan, Occupied Palestinian Territory (Gaza) and Oman as well as among certain Kurdish communities in Iraq (UNFPA 2007: pp. 1-2).

Scenario in sub-Saharan Africa

The practice of FC/FGM is prevalent in 28 African countries in sub-Saharan and North-eastern regions. Estimates at the national level appear that the practice of FC/FGM has found mostly in 28 countries of Africa. Recent estimates indicate that prevalence rate in 18 African countries differs country-wise. The prevalence rate is 90 per cent or higher in countries like Egypt, Eritrea, Mali and Sudan, and less than 50 per cent in Central African Republic and *Cote d'Ivoire,* five per cent in Demographic Republic of Congo and Uganda. There are huge differences in prevalence within countries. Likewise in regions of Mali- in Bamako, the prevalence rate is 95 per cent, while in Koulikoro it is 99 per cent (Rahman and Toubia 2000: p. 7).

FC/FGM in Ethiopia

Ethiopia is one of the African countries where the practice of FC/FGM is widespread. Ethiopia ranks second in population scale in sub-Saharan Africa and have a population of 74 million people. Among that 84 per cent of the population live in rural areas. Many Ethiopian young people face problems in different sectors like education, standard of living and health issue as well (UNFPA and Population Council 2010: p. 1).

Socialisation in large part of Ethiopia is done in a way where girls are considered inferior and subordinate to boys (Ethiopian Society of Population Studies 2008: p. 16). The practice of FC/FGM is a major problem faced by women and girls in Ethiopia. History traces that along with male circumcision FC/FGM emerged in Ethiopia with the coming of Judaic practices a few centuries before the birth of Christ. In the Afar region of Ethiopia, it is considered to have been introduced by the arrival of Ancient Egyptians with who the

Afar was in close contact (Kwaak and Schuringa 2006: p. 47).

In Ethiopia, 80 per cent and in some parts upto 100 per cent women and girls are mutilated as a means of loyalty to their culture and faith (Ethiopian Society of Population Studies 2008: p.18). According to 2005 report, about 74 per cent of Ethiopian women have undergone some form of FC/FGM (UNFPA and Population Council 2010: p. 2).

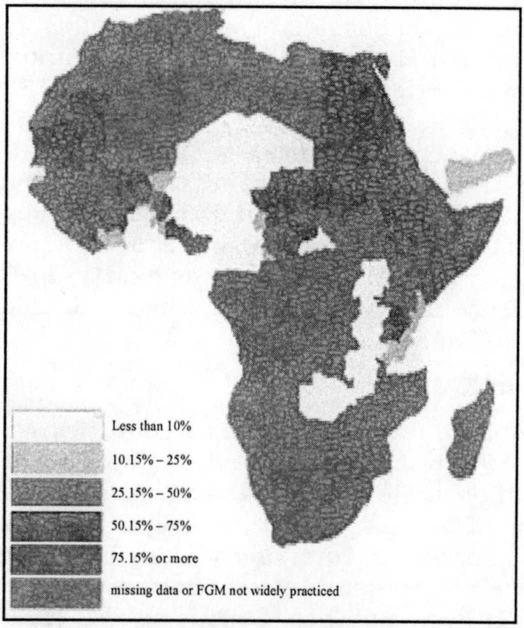

Fig. 1.1: Prevalence of FC/FGM in Africa and Yemen (women aged 15-49).

Source: WHO 2012.

Multiple Indicator Cluster Surveys (MICS), Demographic and Health Survey (DHS) and other national surveys 1997-2006. Map developed by United Nations Children's Fund (UNICEF), 2007.

The map explains the prevalence of FC/FGM on the national survey based on women aged 15-49 years. The prevalence differs widely both between and within the regions and countries with ethnicity as the most important factor. The map shows that in seven countries "the national prevalence is almost universal (more than 85 per cent); four countries have high prevalence (60–85 per cent); medium prevalence (30–40 per cent) is found in seven countries, and low prevalence, ranging from 0.6 per cent to 28.2 per cent, is found in the remaining nine countries. However, the national averages hide the often marked variation in prevalence in different parts of most countries" (WHO 2012).

Table 1.1: FC/FGM Prevalence among Women Aged 15-49, Country-wise

Country	*Survey Type and Date*	*National Prevalence FC/FGM in percentage*
Benin	DHS 2001	17
Burkina Faso	DHS 2003	77
Central-African Republic	MICS 2000	36
Chad (provisional)	DHS 2004	45
Cote d'Ivoire	DHS 2005	42
Djibouti	PAPFAM 2002	98
Egypt*	DHS 2005	96
Eritrea	DHS 2002	89
Ethiopia	DHS 2005	74
Ghana	DHS 2003	5
Guinea	DHS 2005	96
Kenya	DHS 2003	32
Mali	DHS 2001	92
Mauritania	DHS 2000/2001	71
Niger	DHS 2006	2
Nigeria	DHS 2003	19

(Contd...)

(Contd Table 1.1)

Senegal	DHS 2005	28
Sudan*+	MICS 2000	89
Uganda	DHS 2006	1
U.R. Tanzania	DHS 2004/2005	15
Yemen*	DHS 1997	23

*Sample consisted of **ever-married** women ages 15-49
Surveys were conducted in northern Sudan with samples consisting of ever-married women ages 15-49.
Sources: UNICEF, DHS, Pan Arab Project for Family Health (PAPFAM).
Source: UNFPA 2007: p. 2.

* **Ever married** means the men and women who have married once at least in their lives even though their current marital status may not be married but in this above table it includes women.

Table 1.1 above shows the prevalence of FC/FGM in 21 countries on the African continent. There are some countries like Democratic Republic of Congo, Djibouti, Gambia, Guinea Bissau, Liberia, Sierra Leone, Somalia and Togo where FC/FGM is practiced but still DHS or MICS are not conducted (UNFPA 2007: p. 2).

FC/FGM is Practiced by Different Religions

There are various religions that practice FC/FGM. These are Muslims, Christians (Catholics, Protestants and Copts), and Animists as well as non-believers in the specific countries (WHO 2001: p. 37).

Various Tools Used During the Procedure of FC/FGM

There have been various tools used during the procedure of FC/FGM. These tools are non-sterilised as well as this procedure is carried out without anesthesia which results into harmful consequences and serious repercussions on health and mental well-being.

Fig. 1.2: Tools used to perform FC/FGM.

Source: Women's UN Report Network 2012.

FC/FGM is Performed Among Different Age Groups

There is a wide variation in the age at which FC/FGM is performed. It depends on different ethnic groups and locations. Sometimes it is performed when a girl is born or later during adulthood. For example, in Eritrea small baby girls are excised on the seventh day after birth. Most commonly this practice is performed at the age of four and ten or later during adolescence. It is also performed later at the time of marriage (or subsequent marriages), or during a first pregnancy or even during labour time, if not performed earlier (WHO 2001: p. 34).

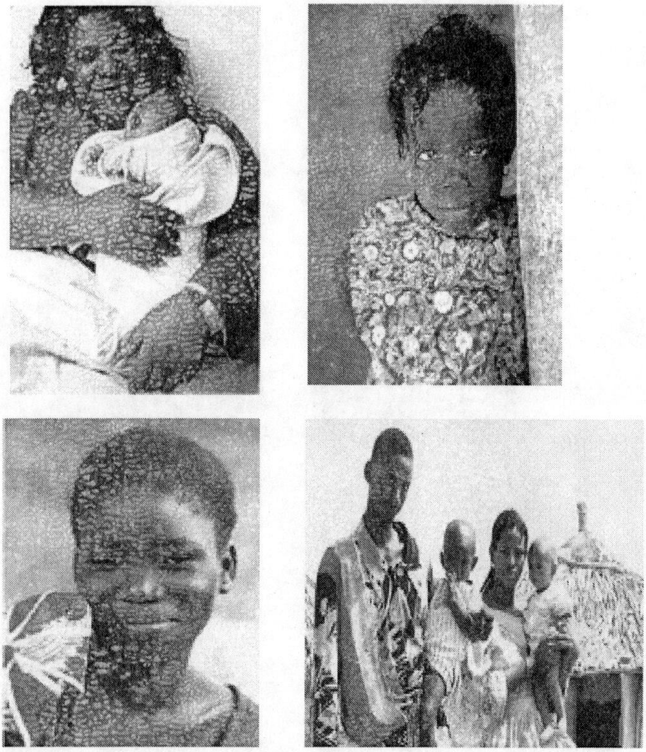

Fig. 1.3: FC/FGM is performed among different age groups.

Source: WHO: 2001 pp. 34-35.

Various Excisors Perform FC/FGM on Women and Girls

The practice of FC/FGM is performed by traditional excisors usually by elderly women in the community. At times, birth attendants or village barbers perform this duty (*ibid:* p. 37).

The New trend "Medicalisation" of FC/FGM

"Medicalisation" of FC/FGM refers to circumstances whereby the process of FC/FGM is performed on woman or a girl by health-care provider in a public or a private clinic, at home or somewhere else. This also includes the procedure of reinfibulation (it is a process performed on women who have undergone type-III category of FC/FGM. This is done by re-suturing (to re-stitch wound or tissue) and recreating an infibulation following a procedure in which the infibulation has been partially or fully opened, generally to make it easier during child birth). Certain health-care providers also contend that the woman who has already undergone FC/FGM; reinfibulation will not cause more harm. This procedure can be undertaken by women during any phase of life (WHO 2010: pp. 2, 8).

The definitions of FC/FGM and "medicalisation" were first adopted in the document *Female Genital Mutilation: A Joint WHO/ United Nations Children's Fund (UNICEF)/ United Nations Population Fund (UNFPA)*, the first statement published by WHO in 1997, and second statement published by WHO was reaffirmed in 2008 by 10 United Nations agencies in the document entitled, *Eliminating Female Genital Mutilation: An Interagency Statement* (*ibid:* p. 2).

The procedure of FC/FGM is usually undertaken by traditional practitioners, parents who want their daughter to undergo this practice as well as women themselves or family members, frequently choose health-care providers to conduct FC/FGM, as they believe this may cause less harm after this procedure rather than done by traditional practitioners. This is the reason for the increased call for health-care providers to perform FC/FGM as people are more aware of the harmful effects on health due to FC/FGM (*ibid:* p. 7).

There have been various reasons for health-care providers to perform FC/FGM. These include:

- Most of the health-care providers who perform FC/ FGM themselves belong to the FC/FGM practicing community in which they provide service.
- They perform FC/FGM based on the request from others to perform the procedure.
- In some countries, health-care providers consider the practice of FC/FGM as medically required for

most women, and some of them consider the practice as harmless.

- At times, some health-care providers, who oppose FC/FGM, continue to believe that it is their duty to support the patient's socio-cultural need to practice FC/FGM.
- Some of the health-care providers say that "medicalisation" of FC/FGM leads to less harm and danger than done by traditional practitioners.
- Eventually, some health-care providers perform it for monetary reasons (*ibid*).

The ongoing practice of FC/FGM on women and girls by the health-care providers creates a sense of legitimacy for the practice. It seems that the practice is harmless. This may lead to the institutionalisation of the practice and may even spread to other cultural groups who do not practice FC/FGM. The "medicalisation" of FC/FGM may lead to the continuation rather than the abandonment of this practice. Though globally FC/FGM is a violation of human rights, "medicalisation" of FC/FGM practiced by health-care providers is breaking their ethics. As in most of the countries, the practice of FC/FGM is a violation of law (*ibid:* pp. 8-9).

Various Reasons for the Cause of FC/FGM

There are various reasons for the continuation of the practice of FC/FGM. Some reasons are as follows:

Socio-cultural Reasons

It is believed that unless a girl is circumcised she would not be considered as mature enough and could not get entry in her age group and be accepted by her ancestors. There is a belief that a woman's external genitalia has the power to blind anyone and when she conceives a baby it may cause physical harm, madness and may lead death of her child and husband. Virginity is a key factor for practicing FC/ FGM which also maintains family's pride and prestige. Patriarchy is the root cause due to which women are forced to practice FC/FGM. Marriage of a girl only takes place if a girl is circumcised. Due to this, girls are under continuous pressure for the practice to be undertaken to avoid facing rejection among their peers and family (WHO 2001: pp. 37-38).

Spiritual and Religious-based Reasons

In various societies FC/FGM is performed on religious grounds. It is compulsory for a girl to undergo this practice to make sure she is spiritually pure and clean though clearly the holy Quran or the Bible do not mention FC/FGM (*ibid:* p. 38).

Psycho-sexual Reasons

There is a belief that if a girl is not circumcised, she tends to be over-active sexually and can easily loose her virginity and may let down her family's honour and reduce chances of her marriage. It is also believed that if a girl is circumcised she will fulfil her husband's sexual pleasure and will maintain a smooth marital life. This practice may also solve the problem of infertility among women (*ibid*).

Hygienic and Aesthetic Reasons

Communities believed that if a girl is not circumcised she is considered to be defiled and impure. Undergoing this practice will make her clean and beautiful (*ibid*).

Socio-economic Factors

It is believed that FC/FGM is necessary and needs to be performed by women before marriage. As women are highly dependent economically on men and the only way for them to get economic support is through marriage, girls are compelled to undergo this practice. The most shocking thing is that women themselves want to perpetuate this practice because they feel it is passed on from generations and it needs to be continued to maintain their culture. At times, women are not aware about the consequences they will face by performing FC/FGM. They blindly continue to practice FC/FGM for their family's honour, to be faithful to their husband as well as maintain their virginity. Another important factor for the continuation of FC/FGM is that it is a source of income for circumcisers, who perform this practice on women and girls (UNFPA 2007: pp. 4-5).

Impact of FC/FGM

The practice of FC/FGM may lead to short-term, long-term, sexual complications and lifelong psychological effects as well as increased risk of Human Immunodeficiency Virus (HIV) on women. The effects of FC/FGM depend on which type of FC/FGM is performed on women, who performed on her and on the level of hygiene condition under which the practice was performed. It also majorly depends on girls and women's health condition and the power to bear the pain while undergoing this practice. Complications usually occur in all types of FC/FGM but the chances of complications are more in case of infibulation. This may lead to severe consequences on physical health and hazardous medical complications as this practice is undertaken with little or no anesthesia (*ibid:* pp. 3-4). There can be short- and long-terms physical complications of FC/FGM.

The Short-term Physical Complications

The short-term physical complications after undergoing FC/FGM are "severe pain, injury to the adjacent tissue of urethra, vagina, perineum and rectum, haemorrhage, shock, acute urine retention, fracture, infection and failure to heal" (WHO 2001: p. 44).

The Long-term Physical Complications

The long-term physical complications after undergoing FC/FGM are "difficulty in passing urine, recurrent urinary tract infection, pelvic infection, infertility, keloid scar, abscess, cysts and abscesses on the vulva, clitoral neuroma, difficulties in menstrual flow, calculus formation in the vagina, Vesico-Vaginal Fistula (VVF), Recto-vaginal Fistula (RVF), problems in child-birth and failure to heal" (*ibid).*

FC/FGM may Cause HIV

The Support for Analysis and Research in Africa (SARA) conducted a project which was researched by experts and scholars regarding the link between FC/FGM and increased risk of HIV infections (Thein 1995: p.1).

But this research is based only on literature review no scientific explanation is available to support it (*ibid*: p. 3). Some of the hypothetical statements regarding the link between FC/FGM and risk of HIV are due to:

- Contaminated instruments in mass circumcision,
- Repeated exposure to the practice,
- Damaged, disrupted tissue,
- Wound infection,
- Repeated reproductive tract infections,
- Dyspareunia, and
- Dry sex (*ibid:* pp. 4-5).

The Psychosocial Consequences of FC/FGM

FC/FGM may lead to serious consequences on the mental well-being of women and girls. Fear, submission, inhibition and the suppression of feelings are likely to occur. This fearful practice is unforgettable. Some women have shared their oppression and reported that they have undergone painful sexual intercourse and menstrual problems after undergoing this practice. These women have accepted this practice as they believe there is no way out rather than accepting as a part of their life. They do not receive any support from their family or friends which may lead to lifelong impact on their mind. Many girls have reported problems with regard to "mental and psychosomatic disorders like eating and sleeping habits, and in mood and cognition. Symptoms include sleeplessness, nightmares, loss of appetite, weight loss or excessive weight gain, as well as panic attacks, difficulties in concentration and learning, and other symptoms of post-traumatic stress. As they grow older, women may develop feelings of incompleteness, loss of self-esteem, depression, chronic anxiety, phobias, panic or even psychotic disorders". The girls who have not undergone may feel constant fear of rejection, social stigma as well as problems in getting a life partner (WHO 2001: pp. 44-45).

Sexual Complications of FC/FGM

The practice of FC/FGM may lead to several sexual problems like painful sexual intercourse due to "scarring, narrowing of the vaginal opening, obstruction of the vagina due to elongation of labia minora and complications such as infection. Severe problems may also occur like vaginal penetration may be difficult or even impossible without tearing or re-cutting the scar" *(ibid*: p. 45).

These above complications have severely affected the health and mental well-being of women and girls and have been a cause of lifelong pain and fear. The tables below will highlight how education can help reduce the practice of FC/FGM.

Table 1.2: Prevalence of FC/FGM among Eldest Daughters by Mother's Education

Survey	*Illiteracy*	*Primary*	*Secondary*	*Total*	*Number of Mothers*
Eritrea 1995	73.7	64.7	59.9	71.4	2,005
Sudan (Northern) 1989-90	62.7	57.2	30.5	57.7	4,386
Mali 1995-96	73.6	73.6	75.0	73.6	6,399
Burkina Faso 1998-99	47.3	35.1	16.1	45.5	3,499
Niger 1998	16.3	6.7	2.2	14.2	1,348
Cote d'Ivoire 1998-99	36.0	9.3	3.9	25.8	1,595
Nigeria 1999	14.6	29.2	23.3	20.2	4,503
Kenya 1998	23.2	10.4	5.8	11.3	4,554
Tanzania 1996	10.7	4.8	0.5	6.7	4,753

Source: Yoder, Abderrahim and Zhuzhuni, 2004: p. 29.

This table shows women with at least one living daughter, percentage of eldest daughters circumcised, by mother's education level (DHS surveys 1989-1999).

The above table shows the correlation between mothers level of education and FC/FGM prevalence rates among eldest daughters in eight countries. It shows, there are major differences in most countries in the case of eldest daughters circumcised depending upon their mother's education level. There is a direct correlation in general between the level of education and the prevalence of FC/FGM. In case of mothers with no education, there may be a high prevalence of FC/FGM among daughters as compared to mother's who have attained secondary education (Yoder, Abderrahim and Zhuzhuni, 2004 : p. 28).

However, there is a direct correlation between high-level of education and low prevalence of FC/FGM. But it cannot be generalised and this relationship does not apply to all the countries under study. For example, FC/FGM is practiced among Yoruba groups in Nigeria (1999), despite the fact that they are educated. Ethnicity is one of the factors for the prevalence of FC/FGM which leads to inconsistencies in the relationship between education level and rate of prevalence *(ibid).*

While in case of Mali (1995-96), there may be an overall low level of education in the country where 81 per cent of respondents had never attended school, and only seven per cent of them attained some secondary education so there are chances of high prevalence of FC/FGM among daughters (*ibid*).

Table 1.3: Prevalence of FC/FGM among Daughters by Mother's Education

Survey	*Illiteracy*	*Primary*	*Secondary*	*Total*	*Number of Mothers*
Egypt 1995	59.5	60.5	22.1	49.7	10,840
Egypt 2000	64.7	62.6	21.2	49.5	11,540
Eritrea 2002	67.5	59.4	40.0	62.5	4,604
Ethiopia 2000	55.7	35.4	25.4	51.8	7,659
Guinea 1999	54.7	44.0	55.1	53.9	4,275
Mali 2001	73.1	73.9	64.8	72.8	8,094
Mauritania 2000-2001	77.4	60.6	41.1	70.9	3,606
Benin 2001	11.1	2.5	0.7	8.2	2,759
Yemen 1997	41.4	23.9	29.0	38.3	4,032

Source: Yoder, Abderrahim and Zhuzhuni, 2004: p. 29.

The Table 1.3 shows women with at least one living daughter, the percentage, who had at least one daughter circumcised, by mother's education (DHS 1995-2002).

The Table 1.3 shows the correlation between mother's level of education and the number of daughters circumcised (may be one or more than that).

The data in Table 1.3 are similar but not equal to the data in Table 1.2. Table 1.2 indicates mother's education and "eldest daughters" circumcised. While Table 1.3 talks about "any of your daughters" circumcised, this may include more than one daughter not only the "eldest daughter". The actual prevalence rate in Table 1.2 must be slightly lower than the figures found in Table 1.3, because some of the youngest daughters may get cut later (Yoder, Abderrahim and Zhuzhuni, 2004: p. 29).

These two Tables 1.2 and 1.3 clearly show that higher level of education may result into decline of the practice of FC/FGM in general.

The above discussion indicates that there is a sharp gender differences between male and female circumcision. A male circumcision is understood to affirm superiority and manhood whereas female circumcision affirms her role in society by controlling her sexual desires and undergoing the rites of passage. Through FC/FGM, a woman maintains her family's honour and fulfils the social norms for acceptance as a part of the community and society.

Though the holy Bible and the Quran strictly discourage or prohibit their followers to initiate FC/FGM, still it is practiced. The "medicalisation" of FC/FGM has become a way for the continuation of this practice as the families feel that this will lead to less pain as it will be performed under hygienic procedure and thus, prevent the health complications, which is normally the case when circumcision is done in a traditional way. However, this cannot be generalised as complications do take place under procedure performed under "medicalisation". The main point is that "medicalisation" provides a justification for the continuation rather than eliminating FC/FGM, which is not the desired objective.

Education plays an important role in minimising the practice of FC/FGM. The statistical data in this chapter shows that the higher the level of education for a mother the lower is the prevalence rate of FC/FGM in general. However, this correlation does not exist uniformly throughout countries in Africa and there are interesting exceptions as in case of Nigeria. Though, the Yoruba women are educated, there is a high prevalence of FC/FGM based on social norms among those of the Yoruba ethnicity.

The following chapter discusses various case studies about women in Ethiopia, who have blindly aped the established cultural norm of FC/FGM and the severe consequences they have faced because they adopted this entrenched cultural practice. It also studies various interesting case studies of opposition to this practice due to increased education and awareness led by various organisations.

References

Dubois, Nicole (2003) *Socio-cognitive Approach to Social Norms,* London and New York: Routledge Taylor and Francis [Online], Available at: <http://books.google.co.in/books?hl=en&lr=&id=7C3idYDvBW4C&oi=fnd&pg=PP1&dq=books+on+social+norms+&ots=OJnw9E7zf7&sig=giko5R7SeFbXIvasEjQYKZjg_I#v=onepage&q=books%20on%20social%20norms&f=false>(Accessed on 30/12/ 2012).

Ethiopian Society of Population Studies (2008). *Gender Inequality and Women's Empowerment: In-depth Analysis of the Ethiopian Demographic and Health Survey 2005,* Addis Ababa: UNFPA [Online], Available at: <http://ethiopia.unfpa.org/drive/Gender.pdf>(Accessed on 17/5/ 2012).

Momoh, Comfort (2005) *Female Genital Mutilation,* Oxon: Radcliffe Publishing [Online], Available at: <http://books.google.co.in/books?id=dVjIPORfVAMC&printsec=frontcover&dq=comfort+momoh&hl=en&sa=X&ei=6H90T_jqO4jirAe385HQDQ&ved=0CDIQ6AEwAA#v=onepage&q=comfort%20momoh&f=false> (Accessed on 23/7/ 2012).

Rahman, A. and Toubia, N. (2000). *Female Genital Mutilation: A Guide to Laws and Policies Worldwide*, London: Zed Books [Online], Available at:<http://books.google.co.in/books?hl=en&lr=&id=kEG6GaudxQEC&oi=fnd&pg=PR 8&dq= history+of+female+genital+mutilation&ots=e74EjotccQ&sig=UD32rEFAdxnY6oWfu_UFqQVKGQ4#v=onepage&q=history%20of%20female%20genital%20mutilation&f=false>(Accessed on 19/6/ 2012).

Sehin, T. (2006) "Tackling Tradition: Examining Successful Strategies in the Mitigation of Female Genital Mutilation in Ethiopian Communities". In Kwaak, A. and Schuringa, M.W. *Gender, Society and Development Gender and Health: Policy and Practice: A Global Source book*, Amsterdam: KIT (Royal Tropical Institute) and London: Oxfam GB, pp. 45-53 [Online], Available at: <http://www.kit.nl/net/KIT_Publicaties_output/ShowFile2.aspx?e=923>(Accessed on 15/6/2012).

Thein, M. (1995). *Female Genital Mutilation and the Risk of HIV*, SARA Issues Paper, Washington: Academy for Educational Development, pp. 1-12.

UNFPA (2007). *A Holistic Approach to Abandonment of Female Genital Mutilation/Cutting*, New York: UNFPA [Online], Available at: <http://www.unfpa.org/webdav/site/global/shared/documents/publications/2007/726_filename_fgm.pdf>(Accessed on 12/4/ 2012).

UNFPA and Population Council (2010). *Ethiopia Young Adult Survey: A Study in Seven Regions*, New York: UNFPA [Online], Available at: <http://ethiopia.unfpa.org/drive/EthiopianYoungAdultSurvey2010.pdf>(Accessed on 12/6/2012).

UNICEF (2013). *Female Genital Mutilation/Cutting: A Statistical Overview and Exploration of the Dynamics of Change*, New York: UNICEF [Online], Available at: <http://www.childinfo.org/files/FGMC_Low_Sept2013.pdf> (Accessed on 18/10/ 2013).

WHO (2001). *Female Genital Mutilation: Integrating the Prevention and the Management of the Health Complications into the Curricula of Nursing and Midwifery: A Teacher's Guide*, Geneva: WHO, [Online], Available at: <http://www.who.int/gender/other_health/teachersguide.pdf>(Accessed on 14/4/ 2012).

WHO (2008). *Eliminating Female Genital Mutilation: An Interagency Statement OHCHR, UNAIDS, UNDP, UNECA, UNESCO, UNFPA, UNHCR, UNICEF, UNIFEM, WHO*, Switzerland: WHO [Online], Available at: <http://www.unfpa.org/webdav/site/global/

shared/documents/publications/2008/eliminating_fgm.pdf>(Accessed on 14/7/2012).

WHO (2010). *Global Strategy to Stop Health-care Providers from Performing Female Genital Mutilation UNAIDS, UNDP, UNFPA, UNHCR, UNICEF, UNIFEM, WHO, FIGO, ICN, IOM, MWIA, WCPT, WMA*, Switzerland: WHO [Online], Available at: <http://whqlibdoc.who.int/hq/2010/WHO_RHR_10.9_ eng.pdf> (Accessed on 31/12/2012).

WHO (2012). *Sexual and Reproductive Health: Female Genital Mutilation and Other Harmful Practices,* WHO [Online], Available at: <http://www.who.int/reproductivehealth/topics/fgm/prevalence/en/index.html>(Accessed on 13/6/2012).

Women's UN Report Network (WUNRN) (2012). 'FGM – Female Genital Mutilation -Women and Girls, UN Commission on the Status of Women' CSW 56: New York [Online] Available at: [Online], Available at: <www.wunrn.com/powerpoint/2012/FGM_12_csw.pps>(Accessed on 16/10/2012).

Yoder, P.S., Abderrahim N., and Zhuzhuni A. (2004). *Female Genital Cutting in the Demographic Health Surveys: A Critical and Comparative Analysis,* Calverton : ORC Marco (DHS Comparative Reports No. 7).

marginalised within the country in terms of health and status (Ethiopian Society of Population Studies 2008: p.10).

Reproductive Health

The status of Ethiopia in terms of health is poor even in comparison to low–income countries. Health facilities are abysmal due to unequal distribution between urban and rural areas. Health problems such as anaemia, malnutrition, pregnancy at very young ages, FC/FGM, septic abortions, sexually transmitted diseases (STDs) and Human Immunodeficiency Virus/Acquired Immunodeficiency Syndrome (HIV/AIDS) all contribute to the high maternal morbidity and mortality rates. There are various problems faced by adolescents on their reproductive health are on account of early marriage, unprotected sex, limited parental guidance and lack of employment opportunities and recreational facilities (UNFPA 1998: p. 4).

FC/FGM in Ethiopia

FC/FGM is one of the major problems faced by women and girls in Ethiopia. In 1997/1998 National Committee on Traditional Practices in Ethiopia (NCTPE) conducted a national baseline survey with the aim to reduce HTP. It states that the practice of FC/FGM is prevalent in almost all parts of Ethiopia and out of 82 ethnic groups, 46 ethnic groups practice FC/FGM. The survey showed that 72.3 per cent women and girls have already gone some form of FC/FGM in Ethiopia. In the Afar region of Ethiopia, the prevalence of FC/FGM is about 94.5 per cent, while in the capital Addis Ababa the prevalence rate is around 70.2 per cent (Kwaak and Schuringa 2006: p. 47).

The 2005 report states that 74 per cent of Ethiopian women and girls have undergone some form of FC/FGM (UNFPA and Population Council 2010: p. 2). FC/FGM is also banned by law, namely, the Revised Penal Code of 2005 in Ethiopia, but there are no stated policies to combat this practice (Save the Children 2008).

2 Female Circumcision/ Female Genital Mutilation: A Case Study of Ethiopia

There are gender differences and the challenges faced by women in the male-dominated society of Ethiopia. This chapter also deals with the overall background of Ethiopia and tries to understand the status of women in the country under study through the lens of their educational status, i.e., the level of education among male and female and the urban-rural continuum. It also discusses the nature of FC/FGM in the different regions of Ethiopia. It further highlights various case studies of women and girls, who have been victims of Female Circumcision/Female Genital Mutilation (FC/FGM) due to lack of awareness and education, that has resulted in poor health and the harmful consequences due to this practice. This chapter highlights that because of attainment of a higher education levels and the increased awareness among educated women led by various organisations, there has been a growing opposition to FC/FGM in a country where a large number of women and girls are subjected to FC/FGM.

The Status of Men and Women in Ethiopia

Ethiopia is by and large a patriarchal society where women's position is subordinate to men. Women's and girls are disadvantaged at the level of education, health, human rights; they do not have the right to take decision in the family. Gender discrimination has also drawn them into the vicious circle of violence and harmful traditional practices (HTP), such as FC/FGM, etc. The prevalence of this heinous practice indicates or is reflective of the fact that women are

Reasons for and Against FC/FGM

Table 2.1: Percentage of Girls Supporting and Opposing their Own FC/FGM and Various Reasons by Profile of Respondent

Characteristic	*All Circumcised Girls, (n=2,895)*	*Circumcised Girls, Afar (n=628)*
Support or oppose own circumcision		
Support	41.5	56.7
Oppose	58.5	43.3
Reasons for support*		
Custom and tradition demand	81.3	86.7
Religion demands	14.1	44.0
Cleanliness	14.9	10.3
Better marriage prospects	19.2	2.7
Prevents immorality	3.9	1.4
Other	3.5	1.3
Reasons for opposition*		
Medical complications	50.3	49.4
Tradition lost significance	38.2	43.7
Painful experience	17.7	21.4
Illegal	44.2	18.9
Against dignity of girl	10.5	5.1
Prevents sexual satisfaction	3.5	4.6

Source: UNFPA and Population Council 2010: p. 39. In the table analysed percentages may sum to over 100, as more than one reason is possible.

What is ironical is that several circumcised girls support their own FC/FGM while a larger percentage also opposes this traditional practice. The details are reflected in Table 2.1 above that shows:

- Among the circumcised girls, 42 per cent supported their own circumcision and 59 per cent opposed their circumcision.

- Fifty-seven per cent of circumcised girls in Afar are more likely to support circumcision as compared to general population of circumcised girls.
- Eighty-one per cent girls who supported the practice, the general reason cited to explain circumcision was on the grounds of custom and tradition. In the case of Afar, 44 per cent of girls cited religious reasons for supporting circumcision, and only three per cent of them cited better marriage prospects for supporting the practice. In the general population of circumcised girls, 14 per cent of them gave religion and 19 per cent cited marriage prospects as a reason to support circumcision, and
- Forty nine per cent girls among the general population and 50 per cent of girls in the Afar region opposed circumcision due to the medical complications that arise after this practice. While 44 per cent of Afar girls and 38 per cent of girls among the general population opposed FC/FGM, and stated that this practice had lost its significance. Only 19 per cent of the girls in Afar opposed this practice and believed that circumcision is illegal. Among the general population of girls, 44 per cent of them said that circumcision is illegal and were actively engaged in opposing circumcision (UNFPA and Population Council 2010: p. 39).

FC/FGM and Religious Orientation

FC/FGM is practiced among Orthodox Christian as well as by Muslim Ethiopians, but the prevalent rate is slightly higher among Muslims. On February 2004, in Western Shoa Zone, Oromia, it was reported by community members that in some parts of Ethiopia, Orthodox priests do not baptise girls if they have not been circumcised (Kwaak and Schuringa 2006: p. 48).

Types of FC/FGM Prevalent in Ethiopia

Type I and Type II are the most prevalent form of FC/FGM that comprises 62 per cent of all cases. While three per cent of female population practices the Type III form (infibulation) of FC/FGM. The type of FC/FGM, and the age at which it is performed is different in various regions as well as ethnic groups. For example, in the Afar region of Ethiopia Type III is the most prevalent. In general, Type I and Type II of FC/FGM is performed by the eighth day after birth. While in parts of Oromia region, girls are circumcised between the ages of five to ten and in ethnic group such as Kembatta, girls are circumcised during adolescents, mostly before marriage (*ibid*: p. 47).

Different Ways of Procedure of FC/FGM

There are different procedures in performing of FC/FGM on women and girls depending on different region and ethnic groups. An older woman, who acts as a birth attendant is more likely to perform FC/FGM on women and girls. In parts of Oromia, a feast is prepared by the mother when the procedure of FC/FGM is performed on a girl. While in Kembatta and neighbouring Sidama Zones, during the procedure of FC/FGM the girl is made to sit on a stool with her head and arms kept behind and bridesmaids cover her eyes with both their hands. The process is described thus:

> *The circumciser, sitting or squatting, faces the girl with the cutting instrument. The process is more complicated in case of infibulation. After the clitoris and other parts of the genitalia are carved away by the circumciser, the sides of the labia majora are usually held together and a paste made up of traditional herbs is applied to the wound to promote healing. The thighs are then tied together and the girl is left lying on a mat until the wound has healed. By that time, the vagina opening will be closed except for a tiny opening left for passing urine. The vagina is usually not opened again until the girl gets married when her husband defibulates her using a sharp instrument* (*ibid*: pp. 47-48).

The table ahead will explain the various types of FC/FGM performed by age, urban-rural continuum in various regions of Ethiopia, and the impact of education on the prevalence of FC/FGM.

Table 2.2: Percentage of Females Aged 12–24 who are Circumcised, by Type of Circumcision and Selected Characteristics among Circumcised Girls

Characteristic	*Per cent Circumcised (n=4,789)*	*Clitoridectomy*	*Excision*	*Infibulation*	*Don't Knew*	*Total*
(1)	*(2)*	*(3)*	*(4)*	*(5)*	*(6)*	*(7)*
Age group						
12-14	46.2	61.8	0.6	2.3	35.3	100.0
15-17	55.6	66.8	2.1	1.9	29.2	100.0
18-20	63.6	62.4	3.9	2.8	30.9	100.0
21-24	66.4	69.1	4.3	2.9	23.7	100.0
Residence						
Urban	49.5	62.7	2.7	2.6	32.0	100.0
Rural	63.9	66.2	3.0	2.5	28.3	100.0
Region						
Tigray	32.5	69.5	0.6	0.0	29.9	100.0
Afar	90.3	32.3	9.2	33.0	25.5	100.0
Amhara	44.4	45.5	2.3	0.7	51.5	100.0

(Contd...)

(Contd...)

(1)	*(2)*	*(3)*	*(4)*	*(5)*	*(6)*	*(7)*
Oromiya	77.4	75.6	3.9	0.0	20.5	100.0
Beneshangul-Gumuz	61.2	79.6	3.4	0.0	17.0	100.0
SNNPR	74.6	93.0	1.1	0.2	5.7	100.0
Addis Ababa	43.6	40.5	1.7	0.0	57.8	100.0
Educational Attainment						
No education	66.6	58.0	5.0	5.0	32.0	100.0
Primary	56.7	67.0	2.5	1.5	29.0	100.0
Secondary	50.2	69.6	2.2	0.6	27.6	100.0
University	38.8	69.6	0.0	0.0	30.4	100.0

Source: UNFPA and Population Council 2010: p. 37. In the table the total number of girls in the sample corresponding to each characteristics category. Percentages circumcised in this survey are comparable to those in the Ethiopia Demographic and Health Survey (EDHS) 2005.

The types of FC/FGM by percentage or prevalence are being tabulated in Table 2.2. It reflected one heartening trend that the higher prevalence among older women than among younger generation suggests that the practice is declining and hopefully with the rise in education will be erased over the coming years. The details are as follows:

- The practice of FC/FGM is found more among older age groups as compared to younger age groups, 66 per cent girls circumcised are among age groups 21-24, while 56 per cent of girls circumcised are in the age group of 15-17, which shows that the practice is declining and may be discontinued over the years.
- In Afar, 90 per cent of the girls are circumcised which is higher as compared to the prevalence rate in Oromiya, at 77 per cent and in Southern Nations Nationalities and People's Region (SNNPR) where 75 per cent of the girls are circumcised. The table states that 33 per cent of the girls in Afar are infibulated, which is the most severe form of FC/FGM, and
- There is a direct correlation between education and FC/FGM. Sixty-six per cent of girls who have not attained education are more likely to be circumcised, than the girls (fifty-two per cent) who have attained higher level of education. There are higher chances, at six per cent, for girls have not attained education to undergo infibulations and only one per cent chance of infibulation among girls having attained at least seven years of education (UNFPA and Population Council 2010: p. 37).

It is also crucial to understand that who takes decision for the practice of FC/FGM. Table 2.3 shows the active role of parents in the Afar region that has reportedly the highest levels of prevalence indicating once again that high level of illiteracy among older women is a major cause of perpetration of this tradition.

Table 2.3: Age at FC/FGM Performed, Decision-maker and Profile of Circumciser

Characteristic	*All circumcised girls (n=2,895)*	*Circumcised girls, Afar (n=628)*
Age at circumcision		
Less than 1 year	49.6	81.2
1-5 years	17.3	7.7
6-10 years	24.9	6.1
Over age 10	8.2	5.0
Who decided upon circumcision*		
Mother	76.3	88.2
Father	57.0	70.1
Grandmother/aunt	5.1	3.1
Respondent	3.6	0.3
Other	2.4	0.8
Don't know	16.2	8.7
Profile of circumciser		
Traditional circumciser	60.8	56.9
Traditional birth attendant	5.6	9.9
Relative	5.5	1.9
Other	2.5	0.2
Don't know	25.6	31.1
Context of circumcision		
Alone	55.0	66.3
In a group	37.3	22.7
Don't know	7.7	11.0
Location of circumcision		
Home	67.6	61.7
Another home or home of circumciser	10.0	8.7
Other (e.g., bush, health facility)	3.1	12.3
Don't know	19.3	17.3

Source: UNFPA and Population Council 2010: p. 38.

The above Table 2.3 shows that girls in Afar region are more dependent on their mother's decision for being circumcised than on their father's decision. This shows that a woman is the perpetrator for the continuation of the practice which is due to the prevalence of patriarchy. It also shows that most of the procedures are carried by the traditional circumciser than by health experts. Afar girls performed this practice alone rather than in a group as compared to all circumcised girls.

- The age of circumcision among Afar girls is during infancy, i.e., below the age of one, as compared to the general population of Ethiopian girls.
- Eight-eighty per cent of the mothers are involved in the decision while seventy per cent of the fathers are involved in the decision-making with regard to FC/FGM of the Afar girls. Among the general population of girls in the seven regions of Ethiopia, seventy-six per cent of the mothers were involved in taking decision regarding FC/FGM and fifty-seven per cent of the fathers were involved in taking decision regarding FC/FGM. Decision of relatives did not play a major role for the practice of FC/FGM. Only five per cent of girls reported that their grand-mother or aunt took part in the decision. And four per cent of girls reported they decided to undergo circumcision on their own.
- Sixty-one per cent of circumcisions were performed by the traditional circumciser. Traditional birth attendants and relatives were responsible, at six per cent each for the circumcision performed.
- Fifty-five per cent girls were alone during the procedure being performed, whereas 37 per cent girls were in a group during the procedure being performed (UNFPA and Population Council 2010: pp. 37-38).

It is also important to understand the attitudes and the differences at the level of urban-rural continuum as well as the varied views of girls and boys in the Afar region.

Attitudes Related to FC/FGM by Urban–Rural Residence and within Afar Region

Table 2.4: Personal Opinions about FC/FGM, by Sex, Type of Place of Residence, and in Afar Region

	Males (n=4,679)			*Females (n=4,792)*		
Percentage agreement with the statement	*Urban*	*Rural*	*Afar Reg.*	*Urban*	*Rural*	*Afar Reg.*
Your community expects you to circumcise your (future) daughters	10.3	36.4	59.1	9.9	32.0	40.3
Most boys in your community would not marry an uncircumcised girl	12.6	35.3	52.1	10.1	31.1	30.9
FC/FGM is required by your religion	19.6	27.5	66.0	10.3	20.7	50.7
Not being circumcised is a dishonour for the girl's family	10.7	33.9	54.6	8.8	33.0	37.4
A girl should undergo FC/FGM before she is married	10.4	37.0	52.8	10.3	33.9	41.7

Source: UNFPA and Population Council 2010: p. 40.

Table 2.4 explains the attitudes related to this harmful practice.

Table 2.4 portrays that there are differences in attitudes between urban, rural and in region of Afar. Majority of the rural people as compared to urban people believe that the practice of FC/FGM should continue due to religious expectations.

But there are variations in the thinking among the girls and boys. Boys are more inclined towards the continuation of this practice which shows the patriarchal nature of society. The table shows:

- There are variations in attitudes related to FC/FGM for urban–rural residence and within Afar region.
- One in 10 urban young people believe that their community or religion demands circumcision and it is necessary for a girl to be circumcised before marriage. Whereas one-third of rural young people believe the above views, but there is slight variations in opinion between the men and women.
- In case of the Afar region, 59 per cent of the boys and 40 per cent of the girls believe that their community demands circumcision, and
- Sixty-six per cent boys and 51 per cent girls believe that religion expects circumcision (UNFPA and Population Council 2010: pp. 39-40).

The spread of education and awareness are the two most important factors that will help eradicate this practice of FC/FGM.

Table 2.5 below discusses about the awareness campaigns or messages through print media or audio-visual ways to make people understand the consequences of this practice.

Attitudes for the Future and the Level of Exposure

Table 2.5: Future Intentions Regarding FC/FGM and Exposure to Messages, by Sex, Type of Place of Residence, and in Afar Region

	Males (n=4,679)			*Females (n=4,792)*		
Percentage agreement with the statement	*Urban*	*Rural*	*Afar Reg.*	*Urban*	*Rural*	*Afar Reg.*
Believe that FC/FGM should continue	7.9	32.2	58.0	8.3	29.8	41.1
Will circumcise (future) daughter(s)	6.8	32.3	58.3	7.0	28.7	40.5
Has heard a message related to FC/FGM	72.1	41.8	44.9	77.3	51.3	59.1
Has heard a public pledge against FC/FGM in the last year	14.1	8.2	4.5	11.4	10.5	1.3

Source: UNFPA and Population Council 2010: p. 40.

Table 2.5 shows that more boys than girls in the Afar region supported circumcision and continued this practice. The message about eradicating FC/FGM is heard more often by girls than among boys. The most common way to pass on the message was through the radio rather than other sources which are mentioned below:

- Fifty-eight per cent of the boys and 41 per cent of the girls in the Afar region wanted to circumcise their daughter's in the future, while the same percentage believes that the practice of FC/FGM should continue.
- More than 70 per cent of urban young people have heard a message regarding FC/FGM; while in Afar, 45 per cent of the boys and 59 per cent of the girls have heard messages regarding spreading awareness and advocating the eradication of FC/FGM.
- Radio (60 per cent) and television (28 per cent) were the common means to spread awareness regarding FC/FGM. Other means to educate people, about 17 per cent was through community-based agent (other than health extension worker), 15 per cent of the advocacy was done through health-care providers, and
- Five per cent of the boys in Afar and only one per cent of the girls in Afar girls have heard a public pledge against FC/FGM (not shown in table above) (UNFPA and Population Council 2010: p. 40).

Thus, education plays a vital role in shaping one's mind and way of thinking. Gender inequalities at the level of education are prevalent in Ethiopia. The tables below depict that low levels of education among girls as compared to boys may result in the continuation of higher levels of prevalence of FC/FGM.

Gender Disparities in Access to Education

In Ethiopia, educational data shows that there are variations in educational attainment between urban and rural areas. Secondary education is largely found among the young urban population as compared to the rural youth. There is also a vast gender difference at the level of education among girls and boys (UNFPA and Population Council 2010: p. 2).

also between urban and rural residence. Thirty-four per cent boys cited poverty as a reason for leaving school, while twenty-nine per cent of girls cited marriage as a reason for leaving school, and

- In case of 40 per cent of the rural girl, marriage was cited as the major reason for leaving school. Contrary to popular assumption, only four per cent of the girls dropped out for reasons of pregnancy (UNFPA and Population Council 2010: p. 25).

Table 2.7: Educational Attainment: Mean Years of Schooling Attained among those Aged 15 and above, by Sex, Type of Place of Residence, Age Group and Region

	Males (n=3,181)			*Females (n=3,558)*		
Characteristic	*Urban*	*Rural*	*All*	*Urban*	*Rural*	*All*
Current age						
15-17	7.3	3.6	4.9	6.6	3.7	4.9
18-20	8.0	3.9	5.6	7.0	2.7	4.5
21-24	8.2	3.6	5.8	6.7	2.2	4.3
Region						
Tigray	8.2	3.8	4.5	7.5	3.1	3.9
Afar	5.8	1.7	3.1	4.1	0.9	2.4
Amhara	7.0	3.3	4.3	5.7	2.3	3.4
Oromiya	7.7	3.7	5.1	7.8	3.0	4.9
Beneshangul-Gumuz	6.5	4.7	5.0	4.6	2.8	3.1
SNNPR	8.8	5.6	7.0	7.5	4.2	5.7
Addis Ababa	8.3	—	8.3	6.9	—	6.9

Source: UNFPA and Population Council 2010 p. 26.

The Table 2.7 above details the educational status variation between regions of the country. It shows:

- Higher levels of education among urban boys in SNNPR, Addis Ababa (8.3 years), and Tigray (8.2 years) (mean 8.8 years education).
- Education level is very low among rural girls in Afar (one year) followed by Amhara (2.3 years), and Beneshangul Gumuz (2.8 years).

- Vast gender difference in level of education. In case of Beneshangul Gumuz, there is two years difference between mean educational attainments of boys (five years) as compared to for girls it is (3.1 years) (UNFPA and Population Council 2010: p. 26).

Table 2.8: Gender Attitudes among Young Adults and Parents toward Education, by Sex (Percentage Holding Inequitable Attitudes)

Attitude	*Male youth (n= 4,669)*	*Female youth (n=4,786)*
Agree with "Boys" are better at math than "girls".	48.9	46.1
Agree with "Most girls are lazy in school".	36.2	33.6
Agree with "Girls are not as good as boys in school".	26.1	22.8
Agree with "when a family is poor and cannot send all children to school, boys should be sent before girls".	23.3	19.7
	Fathers (n=947)	*Mothers (n=1,414)*
Agree with "Boys" are better at math than "girls".	39.8	43.5
Agree with "Most girls are lazy in school".	29.3	30.6
Agree with "Girls are not as good as boys in school".	23.0	21.9
Agree with "when a family is poor and cannot send all children to school, boys should be sent before girls".	27.0	25.5

Source: UNFPA and Population Council 2010: p. 27.

Table 2.8 shows the attitude among adults and parents towards education. It shows:

- There were biased attitudes in favour of boys and against girls with regard to their abilities at school and preferences for sending them to school.
- About half of the respondents agreed that "Boys are usually better at maths than girls," and more than one-third of young people agreed that "girls are usually lazy in school".
- Unfair attitudes regarding girls were found more in case among young people than their parents, and
- Parents gave more priority for sending boys to school than the girls in case of financial difficulties (UNFPA and Population Council 2010: p. 27).

The above data in the context of education shows that due to the lack of education and due to gender inequalities that prevails among girls and boys, there are obstacles in the way of spreading awareness against the practice of FC/FGM at the grassroots levels. Local and world organisations that have launched an awareness programme to counter this practice have a slow response in Ethiopia as illiteracy is widespread.

Case Studies of Victims of FC/FGM

The following case studies of various women and girls who have been the victims of FC/FGM are being studied to show that due to social and religious pressure on women and girls they have gone through the practice of FC/FGM against their wishes. Through their personal experience and sufferings we can make out the level of serious physical and psychological consequences faced by them. Few of them still support and are in favour of continuation of this practice on their own daughters under the threat of being secluded from their community and do not want to go against societal norms. Some case studies shows that due to exposure to education and various awareness campaigns has resulted in women participating in the movement for the abandonment of FC/FGM. Some cases studies reflecting the above mention discussion are cited below:

- Case study no. 1: Bogaletch Gebre;
- Case study no. 2: Aregash Agegnehu and her Daughters;
- Case study no. 3: Ms. Shanko;
- Case study no. 4: Hon. Anab Abdulkadir;
- Case study no. 5: Asmah, Deca, Ferhia and Hassina;
- Case study no. 6: Kauser;
- Case study no. 7: Dohra Ali;
- Case study no. 8: 20 year old Ethiopian girl;
- Case study no. 9: Martha.

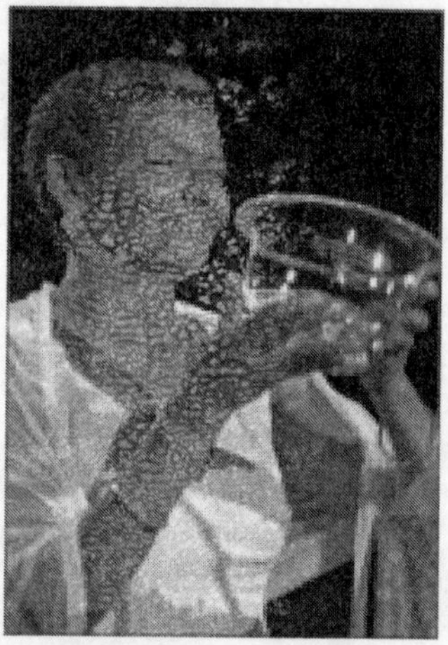

Fig. 2.1: Ms. Bogaletch Gebre.

Source: Gebre 2007.

Case Study no.1: Ms. Bogaletch Gebre is born in rural Ethiopia. She has also gone through the harmful practice of FC/FGM at a very young age and therefore abhors this practice. High levels of educational attainment, her scholarships for an under-graduate degree in microbiology and physiology in Israel, and a PhD in epidemiology in the USA led to an increased awareness, a better understanding of the practice and the desire to change this system. To further her beliefs, while she was a student in California, she set-up a charity called 'Development through Education' and organised marathons to raise money. In total, she sent US$26,000 in the form of technical books, including ones on the subject of health and medicine, to universities and high schools in Ethiopia (Gebre 2007).

In 1997, Gebre founded *Kembatti Mentti Gezzimma* (KMG), a women's self-help centre, in her home village of Kembatta with just US$5000, after winning a European Commission grant for €500,000. KMG was started in four of Ethiopia's eight districts and since then seven and a half districts have declared that they will not support FC/FGM. KMG keeps a record of births, deaths, and also record of girls who have been circumcised or not. National "community conversations" have been launched for the prevention and control of HIV and eradication of FC/FGM in Ethiopia. KMG has played a key role in eradicating the practice of FC/FGM in Ethiopia (*ibid*).

As a result of her contribution to the eradication of FC/FGM, Gebre won the 2007 Jonathan Mann Award for Global Health and Human Rights at the Global Health Council's 34th Annual International Conference on Global Health (*ibid*). She says her dream for African women is:

> *That the world realises that women's suppression is no good for business, for the economy, nor for human development. Africa, in particular, cannot develop unless it uses its entire people. This is what I want to see—a global coalition against gender apartheid* (*ibid*).

Case Study no. 2: Like Gebre, even Aregash Agegnehu, and her two daughters have been victims of FC/FGM. After participating in in-depth community dialogues on the eradication of FC/FGM, Aregash no longer believes that FC/FGM is a requisite part of being women (Tulloch 2009).

Case Study no. 3: Ms. Shanko had performed FC/FGM on girls since past 15 years and she herself had undergone FC/FGM; she lost seven of her nine children in childbirth. As a consequence of a series of educative community dialogues on the physical and psychological harms caused by the practice, she no longer supports FC/FGM. Shanko shared her story with the members of the Pan-African Parliament (PAP) Women's Caucus, which was organised in Addis Ababa to evaluate the status of FC/FGM across Africa and to learn from them. She has also supported various plans and policies that Ethiopia, and other countries have to put forth to abandon the practice of FC/FGM (*ibid*).

Case Study no. 4: Hon. Anab Abdulkadir, is a Pan-African Parliament Acting Chairperson and a member of the Ethiopian Parliament. She underwent FC/FGM as a child. She is now against the practice of FC/FGM. She asked "The demand is coming from where? It is coming from men. If there wasn't a demand, there wouldn't have been any supply. We have to outlaw that demand" (*ibid*).

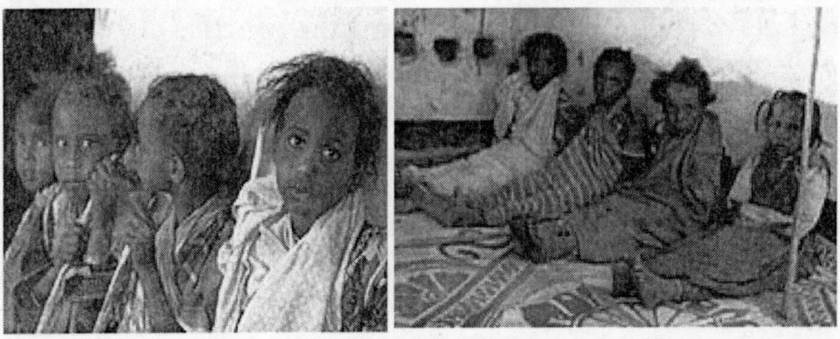

Fig. 2.2: Victims of FC/FGM.

Source: Getachew 2006.

These four girls aged six to eight from the Somali region of Ethiopia – (left to right) Asmah, Deca, Ferhia and Hassina, all underwent FC/FGM and cutting three days before this photo was taken. The girl's legs are tied together to minimise movement after the operation and help heal the wounds.

Case Study no. 5: This case study is about Asmah and her friends. "Like their mothers and grandmothers before them, Asmah and her friends have undergone FC/FGM, a traditional practice that has been going on for thousands of years". Asmah recalls that after undergoing FC/FGM herself, she and her friends were secluded from their community. Their legs were tied together and adults advice them to sleep and not to wash; to help heal their wounds. Before the procedure they were asked to get their hair done, recalled Asmah. They forced them to undergo this practice and tried to comfort them by saying that they would get better after this practice. It caused her a lot of pain and she cried a lot after this practice. Asmah's mother, Bedria Mohammed, was not happy to circumcise her daughter. But she thought that she had no option but has to circumcise her daughter Asmah, otherwise would not get a good husband and a better future. Further, she says that most people in her community believe the practice will guarantee virginity which is required before marriage (Getachew 2006).

Case Study no. 6: Kauser, age18 had gone through the procedure of FC/FGM and says that since she was cut she kept bleeding all the time. She further says that she is afraid of marriage and being again cut (*ibid*).

Dohra Ali with two of her girls, who will remain uncut.

A former circumciser teaching community members on harms of FC/FGM.

Fig. 2.3: Dohra Ali Former Circumciser: Now Preaches Against FC/FGM.

Source: Gelaw 2012.

Case Study no. 7: Dohra Ali, was a former circumciser in the Doho locality in Ethiopia. She said that a campaign to abandon FC/FGM began in the region about that time in 2000. It was mainly led by religious leaders, who tried to explain people that FC/FGM is not expected and supported by Islam. This was good news to many people, who had grown up with the belief that FC/FGM was a religious requirement (Gelaw 2012). The campaign continued for six years, and finally in 2006, in a conference held in Afar, it was decided to totally abandon FC/FGM in the region. "The conference involved senior officials of the regional government, Zonal administrators, *Woreda* (district) and *Kebele* (sub-district) officials and religious and clan leaders. A government regulation reaffirming the Penal Code of Ethiopia (ratified in 2005), which criminalises FC/FGM, was also passed" (Gelaw 2010).

Dohra at first did not the support the campaign but lately she was against the practice when religious leaders held discussions with her community and condemned the practice. When she learned that this practice is not supported by Islam, Dohra decided not to circumcise her five daughters and to do away with her own profession of circumcising girls. She also joined the anti-FC/FGM campaign and decided to educate her daughters (Gelaw 2012).

Case Study no. 8: "In Ethiopia, a 20-year-old woman was thrown out of her home because she refused to be cut. At her wedding, she wore a sign saying, "I am not circumcised. Learn from me". Her husband to-be wore a sign saying, "I am very happy to be marrying an uncircumcised woman". – Info from *New York Times,* 2/6 (Douglas and *et al.* 2003 p. 4).

Case Study no. 9: Martha, a young girl age 15 is from the Danboya Woreda in Ethiopia. She shares her excitement about Whole Body Healthy Life Celebration held in 2004, which she was part of and how it changed her life. She was taught how to speak against FC/FGM and stand proudly with confidence as an unexcised girl. She was one of the few girls to be part of the march at the Whole Body Healthy Life Celebration of 2006. "This celebration was organised independently by Woredas in the Kembatta Zone, [and is a] ground-breaking new rituals marking women's coming of age. These celebrations, which the communities have now taken ownership of, replace the old, harmful practice of removing the dirt (female circumcision) during the harvesting season (The time when women traditionally get circumcised-usually September/October — and are presented to the community as ready for marriage)". She bravely convinced her mother not to circumcise her as well as her younger sister. Through her several trainings in KMG, she learnt about FC/FGM, HIV and general health and nutrition and openly discusses the issue and the harmful practice of FC/FGM with her family and her friends. She feels proud to work towards eradicating FC/FGM. She desires equality, education and most importantly change. She says cultural norms regarding FC/FGM are changing and moving towards eradication (Kembatta Women's Self-Help Centre 2006).

Despite an increase in education, general awareness and an anti-FC/FGM campaign, there are some women who feel that they need to follow the old traditions based on their personal experiences; like in the case of Hodan age 20 has never gone through the procedure of FC/FGM. She does not consider herself lucky because all the girls of her age are married because they have gone through the procedure of FC/FGM. She says that "If she ever has a daughter, she will make sure that she is cut and sealed" (Getachew 2006).

Views of People who have Committed to Eradicate FC/FGM

There is an ongoing movement against the practice of FC/FGM. The message is being passed through poetry, drama and music in the Buremudaytu and Argoba districts in the Afar region in Ethiopia to officially abandon FC/FGM.

The event was attended by government and religious leaders, clan elders, former circumcisers and other community officials was a noteworthy achievement in an area where an extreme form of FC/FGM was a universal practice for centuries in the districts of Amibara, Awash Fentale and Gewane in Ethiopia officially stopped cutting in December 2010 (Gelaw 2012).

A group of girls disavowed female genital mutilation/cutting at a declaration ceremony in the Argoba district.

Fig. 2.4 : Official Declaration to Stop FC/FGM in Argoba District (Ethiopia).

Source: Gelaw 2012.

Voices From the Field Regarding Anti-FC/FGM

FC/FGM violates the right to health, security and physical integrity of the person, the right to be free from torture and cruel, inhuman, or degrading treatment, and the right to life when the procedure results in death. He further added that "Working towards the abandonment of FC/FGM requires a thorough exploration of the beliefs and values that underpin the practice and involving entire communities." ***(Benoit Kalasa, United Nations Population Fund (UNFPA) Country Representative)*** **(UNFPA 2012).**

A new era is dawning for these communities and we urge vigilance in the days and months ahead to make sure that these hard earned commitments are not compromise. ***(Ted Chaiban, United Nations Children's Fund (UNICEF) Country Representative)*** **(UNFPA 2012).**

FC/FGM is against the law. She says here tradition is stronger than the law and she is working with UNICEF to end the practice. ***(Zuleka Ahmed, of the Somali Region Women's Affairs)*** **(Getachew 2006).**

Law enforcement alone can hardly break the deeply rooted tradition. He also says it is necessary to make sure that the legal provisions are there and that people

talk about it." ***(Björn Ljungqvist, UNICEF Representative in Ethiopia)*** **(Getachew 2006).**
From a religious point of view "I would like to inform you that Islam does not allow FC/FGM," he said. "As Muslims, when our religion says you have to abandon this practice, you have to completely abandon it. Otherwise you are not a true believer. ***(The Imam of the village mosque)*** **(Getachew 2006).**
At a declaration ceremony on abandonment of FC/FGM in northern Ethiopia's Awash-Fentale District she said that "It's a huge success to see so many girls here who are proud that they are not circumcised, which would have been considered as a taboo a few years back. ***(Asiya Oumer, Afar Regional Youth Federation representative)*** **(UNICEF 2011).**
He promised to follow in the footsteps of Amibara and Awash-Fentale and declare abandonment of cutting in his district in the near future. ***(Mohammed Asheraye, Administrator of a neighbouring district)*** **(UNICEF 2011).**

Waning of FC/FGM Due to Education and Awareness

FC/FGM is a very sensitive issue to deal with or talking about in many parts of rural Africa where strong oral traditions in support of FC/FGM prevail. Education and various communication techniques are helping to spread awareness regarding the abandonment of FC/FGM, though at a much slower pace than desired (Beatrice and Pamela 1998: p. 44).

The practice of FC/FGM is declining in Ethiopia. The 2005 Demographic and Health Surveys (DHS) report, states that in Ethiopia about 70 per cent of the women interviewed were in favour of discontinuation of the practice as compared to in 2000 DHS report, wherein it was 40 per cent. Discontinuation of FC/FGM has increased since the last two decades. Recently, there are various programmes launched at community level to eradicate FC/FGM in many parts of Ethiopia. There are several ways to eradicate FC/FGM through:

> *Sensitisation and mobilisation of the community through information, education and communication/ behaviour change communication (IEC/ BCC) toward reproductive health issues focussing on HTPs, particularly FC/ FGM, through training of the community members such as community health agents (CHAs), elders, religious and traditional leaders, women with key roles in the community, establishment of anti-FC/ FGM committee and community action team, and provision of training and improving quality of reproductive health services through the camp-based health centre* (Mitike and Deressa 2009: p. 2).

Among the regions of Adere and Oromo, the practice of infibulation has reduced in the recent past due to campaigns by Muslim leaders who are advocating milder type of circumcision. Due to increased awareness through mass media and information given in hospitals, the practice of FC/FGM is now less common among the Adere and Oromo. Marrying a person of their own choice is permissible as well as FC/FGM is now less relevant criteria for marital reasons. However, there are a percentage of men who would still prefer marrying a circumcised woman. Socialisation has played an important role in shaping the attitudes, thought processes of men and women and it their decision to support the practice of FC/FGM or to eradicate it (Missailidis and Medhin 2000: p.137).

Communication and interaction within the community has played a vital role in the eradication of FC/FGM. In early 2009, Consensus Building Conference was held in Afar region where regional; district, and sub-district government and administration officials met together and reached a decision to organise a community talk within their own communities to eradicate FC/FGM. They also took a collective pledge to discontinue the practice and not circumcise their own children as well as draw up legislation after the communities decide to abandon FC/FGM (Gelaw 2010).

The sustained work done by local organisations including the Afar Region Bureau of Women, Children and Youth Affairs, the Afar Pastoralist Development Association (APDA) and the Rohi Weddu Pastoralist Women's Development Organisation since many years has led to collective declarations to eradicate FC/FGM. The immense support of UNFPA-UNICEF Joint Programme to Accelerate Abandonment of FC/FGM, and their aim of changing social norms has been a major reason for the success of the anti-FC/FGM drive (Gelaw 2012).

In the Afar region, the practice of FC/FGM was universal in the past, but slowly the practice is vanishing as social norms are changing in favour of abandoning FC/FGM. The data cited above shows that the rate of uncircumcised girls in Buremudaytu district in Afar has reached upto 1,120, while in Argoba district in Afar all 106 girls born in 2011, remain uncut. Current data shows that the rate of uncut girls in the six Afar districts has increased to 7,000 and in 2010, the rate of uncut girls was only 4,000 (*ibid*).

The chapter examines that Ethiopia being a highly patriarchal society the harmful practice of FC/FGM still prevails. The reflection that FC/FGM's prevalence is higher in the Afar region as compared to other regions of Ethiopia is of significance. In the Afar region, the factors that contribute to the continuation of FC/FGM and the reasons for a higher prevalence rate are; high levels of illiteracy, pressure on religious grounds and mother's decision to circumcise their daughters. In the other regions, in relative terms, there is a higher level of literacy and lesser pressures on religious grounds or women decision-making in favour of FC/FGM. And therefore the prevalence rates are comparatively lower among the other ethnic groups outside of the Afar region.

There are variations of prevalence in the context of urban-rural continuum in regions based on the level of education and awareness campaigns. Education, decision-making power, will of parents to practice FC/FGM on their daughters, religious and ethnic orientations that favour FC/

FGM are the main reasons for the high level of prevalence of FC/FGM in the Afar region as well as in other regions of Ethiopia. Through statistical data this study shows the direct one to one correlation between the levels of education in society and the prevalence of FC/FGM, i.e., the higher the level of education the lower would be the prevalence of FC/FGM in the years to come.

Through various case studies from Ethiopia, it showed that those who have undergone FC/FGM have also approved the circumcision of their own daughters and some of them have opposed subsequently due to an increase in their level of awareness due to higher education. Several women who were victims of FC/FGM at a young age and received higher education at home and abroad are now raising awareness and fiercely fighting against the practice of FC/FGM. Through their awareness programmes they are working hard towards the abandonment of this practice for a better future of women in Ethiopia. Also the sustained efforts of various organisations and NGOs have helped in minimising the practice.

FC/FGM is a severe violation of human rights of women. The initiatives taken by organisations and various campaigns and measure taken at national level to curtail this practice of FC/FGM will be discussed in the following chapter.

References

Beatrice, S. and Pamela N. (1998). "Campaigning Against Female Genital Mutilation in Ethiopia Using Popular Education", *Gender and Development,* Vol. 6 (2), London and New York: Taylor and Francis, pp. 44-52 [Online], Available at:<http://www.jstor.org/stable/4030344> (Accessed on 20/5/ 2012).

Douglas and *et al.* (2003) "Ethiopia: African Women Meet to Oppose Genital Mutilation", *News Africa,* Vol. 33 (3-4), Washington: Off Our Backs, p. 4 [Online], Available at:<http://web.ebscohost.com/ehost/pdfviewer/pdfviewer?vid=5&hid=8&sid=80cef024-b566-47b0-b06d-d80796e06aee%40sessionmgr13> (Accessed on 20/5/2012).

Ethiopian Society of Population Studies (2008). *Gender Inequality and Women's Empowerment: In-depth Analysis of the Ethiopian Demographic and Health Survey 2005*, Addis Ababa- UNFPA [Online], Available at: <http://ethiopia.unfpa.org/drive/Gender.pdf> (Accessed on 17/5/2012).

Gebre, B. (2007). 'Ending Female Genital Mutilation in Ethiopia', *The Lancet*, Vol. 369 (9579) p. 2071 [Online], Available at: <http://www.lancet.com/journals/lancet/article/PIIS0140-6736 (07)60964-7/fulltext> (Accessed on 22/4/2012).

Gelaw, A. (2010). *Abandoning Female Genital Cutting/Mutilation in the Afar Region of Ethiopia,* UNFPA [Online], Available at: <http://www.unfpa.org/public/news/pid/5141> (Accessed on 22/4/2012).

Gelaw, A. (2012). *Two More Corners of Ethiopia Call for an End to Genital Cutting,* UNFPA [Online], Available at: <http://www.unfpa.org/public/home/news/pid/9964> (Accessed on 22/4/ 2012).

Getachew, I. (2006). *Battling an Ancient Tradition: Female Genital Mutilation in Ethiopia,* UNICEF [Online], Available at: <http://www.unicef.org/infobycountry/ethiopia_34881.html> (Accessed on 22/4/2012).

Kembatta Women's Self-Help Center (2006). *Whole Body Healthy Life 2006: Freedom from Female Genital Excision (FGE),* Addis Ababa: Ethiopia [Online], Available at: <https://docs.google.com/viewer?a=v&pid=gmail&attid=0.1&thid=1393e315d1e5c561&mt=application/pdf&url=https://mail.google.com/mail/?ui%3D2%26ik%3D595b2e0693%26view%3Datt%26th%3D1393e315d1e5c561%26attid%3D0.1%26disp%3Dsafe%26realattid%3Df_h61wt8cf0%26zw&sig=AHIEtbRPC7RSqczo9WkI7md1O23SL6f1xQ>(Accessed on 19/8/ 2012).

Mitike, G. and Deressa, W. (2009). "Prevalence and Associated Factors of Female Genital Mutilation among Somali refugees in Eastern Ethiopia: A Cross-sectional Study", *BMC Public Health,* Addis Ababa: School of Public Health, Vol. 9, pp. 264-273 [Online], Available at:<http://web.ebscohost.com/ehost/pdfviewer/pdfviewer?vid=4&hid=11&sid=80cef024-b566-47b0-b06d-d80796e06aee%40sessionmgr13> (Accessed on 20/5/2012).

Missailidis, K. and Medhin- Gebre, M. (2000). "Female Genital Mutilation in Eastern Ethiopia", *Lancet*, Vol. 356 (9224), Uppsala: Department of Women's and Children's Health, International Child Health, p.137 [Online], Available at:<http://web.ebscohost.com/ehost/pdfviewer/pdfviewer?vid=4&hid=8&sid=80cef024-b566-47b0-b06d-d80796e06aee%40sessionmgr13> (Accessed on 20/5/ 2012).

Save the Children (2008). *Prevention and Eradication of Female Genital Mutilation (FGM) and other Harmful Traditional Practices (HTPs) in Ethiopia*, Norway-Ethiopia and Partners [Online], Available at:<https://docs.google.com/viewer?a=v&pid=gmail&attid=0.2&thid=1393e315d1e5c561&mt=application/pdf&url=https://mail.google.com/mail/?ui%3 D2%26ik%3D595b2e0693%26view%3Datt%26th%3D1393e315d1e5c561%26attid%3D0.2%26disp%3Dsafe%26realattid%3Df_h61wvjxh1%26zw&sig=AHIEtbQOY1px0K5OltivbMgBblu3DaYV>(Accessed on 19/8/ 2012).

Sehin, T. (2006). "Tackling Tradition: Examining Successful Strategies in the Mitigation of Female Genital Mutilation in Ethiopian Communities". In Kwaak, A. and Schuringa, M. W. *Gender, Society and Development Gender and Health: Policy and Practice: A Global Sourcebook*. Amsterdam: KIT (Royal Tropical Institute) and London: Oxfam GB, pp. 45-53 [Online], Available at: <http://www.kit.nl/net/KIT_Publicaties_output/ShowFile2.aspx?e=923> (Accessed on 15/6/2012).

Tulloch, T. (2009). *In Ethiopia, African Women Parliamentarians Condemn Female Genital Mutilation,* UNICEF[Online], Available at:<http://www.unicef.org/infobycountry/ethiopia_51122.html>(Accessed on 22/4/2012).

UNFPA (1998). *United Nations Population Fund Proposed Projects and Programmes*, UNFPA [Online], Available at: <http://ethiopia.unfpa.org/drive/eth9801.pdf>(Accessed on 27/5/ 2012).

UNFPA and Population Council (2010). *Ethiopia Young Adult Survey: A Study in Seven Regions,* New York- UNFPA [Online], Available at: <http://ethiopia.unfpa.org/drive/EthiopianYoungAdultSurvey2010.pdf>(Accessed on 12/6/2012).

UNFPA (2012). *Two Districts in Afar Region Declare Abandonment of FGM/C*, UNFPA [Online], Available at: <http://ethiopia.unfpa.org/2012/01/24/4476/two_ districts_

in_afar_region_declare_abandonment_of_fgm_c/>(Accessed on 22/4/2012).

UNICEF (2011). *Two Districts in Northern Ethiopia Declare an End to Female Genital Cutting*, UNICEF [Online], Available at: <http://www.unicef.org/infobycountry/ethiopia_57521.html> (Accessed on 22/4/2012).

3 Female Circumcision/ Female Genital Mutilation: National Response from a Human Rights Perspective in Africa

The practice of Female Circumcision/Female Genital Mutilation (FC/FGM) is a violation of human rights. This section deals with the various efforts taken by various organisations and Non-governmental Organisations (NGO) since the beginning of 20th century to eradicate FC/FGM. It studies the initiative taken by the United Nations Population Fund (UNFPA), and United Nations Children's Fund (UNICEF) through the Joint Programme and through the human rights-based approach (HRBA) at community, national and regional level by enacting laws, awareness campaigns, spreading education and creating an environment where people themselves create a change within themselves to eliminate FC/FGM in countries of Africa in general and Ethiopia in particular.

FC/FGM: A Human Rights Violation

On December 10, 1948 the first International Bill of Rights, the United Nations Universal Declaration of Human Rights (UDHR) was adopted, which was unambiguous about the universality of human rights, which included the equal rights of men and women. Article 1 of UDHR proclaims that "All human beings are born free and equal in dignity and rights." This statement was emphasised by Article 2 of the UDHR:

> *Everyone is entitled to all the rights and freedoms set forth in this declaration, without distinction of any kind, such as race, colour, sex, language, religion, political or other opinion, national or social origin, property, birth or*

other status (emphasis added). Furthermore, no distinction shall be made on the basis of the political jurisdiction or international status of the country or territory to which a person belongs whether it is independent, trust, non-self-governing or under any other limitation of sovereignty (Rwomire 2001: p. 70).

Eighteen years after UDHR was born two other international bills of rights were adopted on December 16, 1966. They are the International Covenant on Civil and Political Rights (ICCPR), and the International Covenant on Economic, Social and Cultural Rights (ICESCR). Both these bills stated the equality between men and women (*ibid:* p.70).

FC/FGM is recognised as a harmful practice and a violation of the human rights of women and girls. The legal actions as well as various political documents, obtained from United Nations (UN), world conferences and summits, which assert human rights and addresses governments to take efforts for their full respect, protection and fulfillment that are applicable to FC/FGM as well (WHO 2008: p. 8).

The Former UN Secretary-General, Kofi Annan, on the International Human Rights Day, 10th December 1997 stated that:

Human rights are the expression of those traditions of tolerance in all religions and cultures that are the basis of peace and progress. Human rights are foreign to no culture and native to all nations (UNFPA and Harvard School of Public Health 2010: p. 23).

Concept of Human Rights-based Approach (HRBA)

A HRBA is a conceptual framework for the process of human development that prescribes a norm based on international human rights standards and functions that is regulated towards promoting and protecting human rights. It tries to examine the inequalities which are situated at the innermost of development problems and retrieve discriminatory practices and unfair distributions of power that hinders development progress. "In the HRBA, the plans, policies and processes of development are anchored in a system of rights and corresponding obligations established by international law." This supports to raise the sustainability of development work, enables people themselves in particular the most marginalised to take part in the framing policy and hold responsible to those, who have a duty to act (Office of the United Nations High Commissioner for Human Rights 2006: p.15).

In early 2000, several UN agencies had already adopted a HRBA to development, but they perceived this approach in distinct ways. But due to UN interagency cooperation particularly at country level in the framework of the Common Country Assessment (CCA) and UN Development Assistance Framework (UNDAF), it became obvious that it was crucial to come to a 'common understanding' of what a HRBA means for the work of UN agencies and their partners. The outcome of this was that group of UN agencies came to an agreement regarding the major elements of HRBA. This agreement is known as the 'UN Common Understanding' (UNFPA and Harvard School of Public Health 2010: p.70).

It is important to note that UNFPA pays particular attention to underline linkages between cultural sensitivity, gender-responsiveness, and HRBA. In carrying out HRBA into programming, concerns towards culture and gender are at the leading position of the UN agencies (*ibid*).

Actions Taken to Eradicate the Practice of FC/FGM

The early 20th century brought about the first documented action against the practice of FC/FGM. There is possibility that certain undocumented efforts were also undertaken by the local population for eradicating the practice of FC/FGM much earlier (Rahman and Toubia 2000: p. 9).

In the beginning of 1900s, in countries like Burkina Faso, Kenya and Sudan, initiative were taken by colonial administrations and missionaries to abandon the practice of FC/FGM by enforcing laws and church rules, but they did not succeeded. Instead it involved a backlash and anger against foreign intervention. Similarly, in 1940s and 1950s, in Sudan and Egypt efforts were taken by governments to put forth laws regarding FC/FGM which also failed due to lack of awareness campaigns among people for the opposition of the practice (*ibid:* pp.9-10).

During the 1960s and 1970s, opposition to FC/FGM among people in Africa began. Women's groups in many countries held awareness campaigns regarding the ill-effects of this practice. Moreover, doctors in Nigeria, Sudan and Somalia began to notice and began writing in medical journals regarding the harmful consequences faced by women and girls after this practice (*ibid*: p.10).

In the year 1979, in Khartoum, the capital of North Sudan, the World Health Organisation (WHO) financed the first seminar on Harmful Traditional Practices Affecting the Health of Women and Children. Many women from various African countries attended this seminar and opposed the practice of FC/FGM as well as "medicalisation" of FC/FGM. Moreover, national commissions were also set-up regarding anti-FC/FGM. Even though there was opposition by women regarding the practice of FC/FGM, the medical community in Africa and West continues to medicalise the practice (*ibid*).

Later in 1993, the World Medical Association strongly disapproved "medicalisation" of FC/FGM; along with that several other medical professional associations, namely, the International Federation of Gynaecology and Obstetrics (FIGO), as well as by international agencies, NGOs and governments also disapproved "medicalisation". In addition, this disapproval of "medicalisation" of FC/FGM was also repeated "in the joint *WHO/UNICEF/UNFPA* in first statement against FC/FGM in 1997 as well as in the *Interagency Statement on the Elimination of FC/FGM* that was co-signed by 10 United Nations agencies in 2008. Moreover, many United Nations Treaty Monitoring Bodies *inter alia* the Committee on Elimination of All Forms of Discrimination Against Women (CEDAW), called on countries to eliminate the "medicalisation" of FC/FGM" (WHO 2010: p. 4).

Further in the 1980s, efforts by African women to eradicate the practice of FC/FGM continued. In 1980, an UN Mid-Decade Conference on Women and the NGO Forum was held in Copenhagen, where four African women activist participated in a panel discussion on FC/FGM. In the conference, there were different viewpoints on the subject of eradicating the practice of FC/FGM between the indigenous African women and the Western women. This was perceived by African women as a display of a superior attitude by the Western women towards them. Due to this clash of ideas, an informal and home-grown network of African activists emerged to deal with this practice and work towards its eradication (Rahman and Toubia 2000: p.10).

Likewise in 1984, there was a meeting organised by women of African NGOs in Dakar, Senegal, which led to the birth of the Inter-African Committee (IAC) on Traditional Practices Affecting the Health of Women and Children. Fifteen years after the Dakar meeting, IAC affiliates were established in more than 26 African countries. Since then it helped to educate national governments and also the masses regarding the negative consequences of FC/FGM (*ibid:* p.10).

The year 1980s marked the turning point in the history of FC/FGM. Intellectual thinking regarding FC/FGM by international feminist scholar and advocates was carried out. Scholars started questioning about the unequal human rights laws on the basis of gender. They also enquired about the traditional and human rights law which gave much more emphasis to the "public" sphere, i.e., in the domain of politics, government and the state. Little emphasis was given towards the "private" sphere, i.e., family and society where violence against women frequently takes place. Due to an emphasis on the public sphere rather than private sphere, violence against women such as; domestic violence, dowry deaths, FC/FGM etc. were not considered as violation of women's human rights and the government's remained aloof and silent. (*ibid:* pp.10-11).

Later in 1981, government officials as well as private parties recognised the practice of FC/FGM as violation of women's rights and was made explicit in the CEDAW (*ibid*: p.11).

Further the UN Convention on the Rights of the Child (CRC) in 1989 mentions FC/FGM as a violation of the rights of children. The African Charter on the Rights and Welfare of the Child, passed in 1990, specifically mentions the obligation to protect children from traditional practices that are harmful to health. Article 5 of Maputo Protocol of 2003 (regional instrument named the Protocol of the African Union on the Rights of Women in Africa, commonly known as the Maputo Protocol) states that harmful practices including FC/FGM is a violation of human rights and calls for a ban on these practices. It states that measures should be taken to eradicate them (Deutsche Gesellchaftfur Internationale Zusammenarbeit 2011b).

The era of 1990s marked a distinct African leadership on FC/FGM which gave rise to increase awareness on FC/FGM at international level as well as dealing this practice on the grounds of women's human rights. Various committees were set-up as well as world conferences were held on the subject of FC/FGM. The CEDAW in 1990 referred, in particular, to the practice of FC/FGM under the Women's Convention. Further in 1993, United Nations Declaration on the Elimination of Violence against Women explicitly included FC/FGM within its definition of the phrase "violence against women" (Rahman and Toubia 2000: pp. 11-12).

The international community once more regarded FC/FGM from a human rights perspective in various international conferences which are as follows:

1. The World Conference on Human Rights, in Vienna, 1993.
2. The International Conference on Population and Development (ICPD), in Cairo, 1994.
3. The Fourth World Conference on Women, in Beijing 1995.

These world conferences were attended by a large number of women where women's rights were discussed intensively. During these meetings and the subsequent women's conferences in Beijing, the issue of FC/FGM was at the centrestage. At these gatherings various strategies were drawn up for appropriate policies. Actions taken against FC/FGM were planned and characterised in the final documents which were authorised by the government. The outcome of the women's movement led to the appointment of Radhika Coomerswamy as the Special Rapporteur on Violence against Women by the Commission on Human Rights, in 1994. Various reports under her leadership have focussed on the evil practice of FC/FGM and the efforts that need to be undertaken to eradicate it completely (*ibid*: pp.11-12).

In 1998, at the Council of Ministers during its 68 session, the Addis Ababa Declaration on violence against women was adopted by the Organisation of African Unity (OAU). Further this declaration was also approved by the Assembly of Heads of State and Governments. This declaration was very significant in the formulation of an African Charter on violence against women that gives the framework for national laws against FC/FGM. In 1998, the Banjul Declaration also demanded the abandonment of FC/FGM and other harmful practices during the time when IAC together with Gambian Committee on Traditional Practices (GAMCOTRAP) organised a conference in Banjul, the capital of Gambia (UNFPA 2012).

In 1999, the United Nations Social, Humanitarian and Cultural Committee (Third Committee of the General Assembly), sanctioned a resolution by demanding the state to implement national laws and policies that bans traditional or customary practices including FC/FGM as it affects the health of women and girls. It further requests the state to prosecute anyone who commits such practices on women and girls. The UN organisation also spreads awareness, organises and encourages international and national opinion on the harmful consequences of FC/FGM. In the same year, in 1999, the Ouagadougou Declaration was adopted at a workshop organised by the West African Economic and Monetary Union (UEMOA) at Ouagadougou, the capital of Burkina Faso and demanded the eradication of FC/FGM (*ibid*).

Since 1990s, many African countries have passed laws for banning of FC/FGM. In countries of Burkina Faso (1996), Côte D'Ivoire (1998), Djibouti (1995), Egypt (2008), Ethiopia (2004), Eritrea (2007), Ghana (1994), Guinea (2000), Kenya (2001), Senegal (1999), South Africa (2005) and Tanzania (1998), if anyone practices FC/FGM, it is punishable by law (Deutsche Gesellchaftfur Internationale Zusammenarbeit 2011a).

The constitution of countries of Ethiopia and Ghana prohibits harmful traditional practices (HTP) which also include FC/FGM. In some countries where laws are not passed against FC/FGM, there are regulations included in criminal laws regarding assault and physical harm caused which provide justice to the victim, who have undergone this practice. Though legal action is rarely put forth, sentences against the violators are known to be passed in Burkina Faso, Egypt, Ghana and Senegal. In addition, governments in many African countries have drafted national action plans to abandon FC/FGM and several countries on the continent are in the process of implementing these laws (*ibid*).

In Switzerland and in some EU (European Union) member states, including Belgium, Denmark, the Italy, Norway, Sweden and Spain and United Kingdom, the practice of FC/FGM is banned. In other EU countries, the practice FC/FGM can be punished by law through laws of covering bodily harm and child abuse. Anyone found guilty of an offence have to pay penalty and at times imprisoned. But still in Europe as in Africa, offences are rarely reported. In Germany, the German Network to Overcome FC/FGM (INTEGRA) has framed important elements for a national action plan. These include that FC/FGM is crime in itself, protection of girls who are at risk and women affected by this practice within Germany and increase participation of migrants in ending the practice (*ibid*).

In the year 2000, efforts were taken to implement the Beijing Declaration and Platform for Action. This declaration states the progress made in several national laws towards the banning of FC/FGM. It also talks about the discriminatory attitudes and norms that still continue and make women and girls more prone to gender-based violence including FC/FGM. Further, it also calls upon national governments' actions to eradicate violence against women (UNFPA 2012).

The Millennium Development Goals (MDG), which emerged out of the United Nations Millennium Declaration, was implemented in the year 2000 by 189 Member States. It provided the current international framework for evaluating growth towards sustainable development and eradicating poverty. One of the major objectives of the MDG was to promote gender equality and empower women, and to abandon FC/FGM, as this practice has serious repercussions on women's and girl's sexual and reproductive health (WHO 2010: p. 6).

Due to growing migration from Africa to other parts of the world there are many immigrant and refugee service organisations for African immigrant communities to deal with the issue of FC/FGM. Recently, there have been many developments by African organisations including women's NGOs that deal with the issue of health, human rights and the abandonment of FC/FGM. These organisations have received funds from many national and international organisations and technical agencies like WHO, UNICEF and UNFPA. There have been enormous changes in the practice of FC/FGM due to new techniques to increase awareness. These techniques are used to spread anti-FC/FGM messages through music, theatre, films and radio, awareness campaigns, education as well as workshops at community, national and international levels. Along with that various laws are enacted with regard to anti-FC/FGM in many African countries and have tackled this practice on grounds of human rights to eliminate this practice (Rahman and Toubia 2000: pp. 12-13).

Awareness at National Level to Eradicate FC/FGM

The practice of FC/FGM cannot be dealt in isolation. It is a deeply rooted tradition and there are various factors such as social, cultural and political interlinked together that are responsible for the continuation of this practice. The most important way to eradicate the practice of FC/FGM is to change the mind-set among the people from within. Alongside, public support and their agreement to abandon this practice are crucial factors to bring about long lasting changes (UNFPA and UNICEF 2011: p. 9).

The UNFPA-UNICEF Joint Programme with its holistic, culturally sensitive, participative approach from a human rights perspective has fostered to bring about a positive change towards the eradication of FC/FGM among communities. These two UN agencies have also formed partnerships and collaborations at local, national, regional and global levels, with community and faith-based organisations, religious leaders, safe motherhood projects, NGOs, relevant government ministries and other UN agencies (*ibid:* p. 9).

Various efforts at the community, national as well as regional levels to eradicate the practice of FC/FGM are as follows:

(a) Community Efforts to Eradicate FC/FGM

Education and awareness play a key role in changing the mind-set of a person. Education sessions were organised in 71,245 communities in 12 targetted countries in 2010 led by the Joint Programme regarding anti-FC/FGM. These sessions were carried out for months in each community. About 7,524 of them were trained to monitor sessions. These sessions dealt with various issues like "women's health (anatomy, physiology, reproductive health and immunisation) and hygiene (infection, transmission and prevention). It also highlighted fundamental human rights such as the right to life, to peace and security, bodily integrity, health, the right to be protected against all forms of discrimination, the right to an education, the right to be married, the right to freely express one's opinions and the right to information". More than three million community members consisting of men, women and young people attended the sessions. During these sessions people engaged in group discussions, role playing, theatre, poetry and songs about human rights. Due to these efforts, the perception of people changed and they decided by themselves to keep their daughters uncut (UNFPA and UNICEF 2011: p. 9).

Public pledges also play crucial role in gaining public support in eradicating this practice. In 2010, 596 public celebrations were held to eradicate FC/FGM in some countries. The result of this was that 9,696 families in Egypt and 6,400 families and 52 communities in Sudan eradicated this practice during the same time. In Senegal, 502 public community declarations took place as compared to 256 in 2009. In Gambia, 19 communities publicly declared to eradicate this practice (*ibid*: p.10).

(b) National Level Efforts to Eradicate FC/FGM

In 2010, the Joint Programme together with national stakeholders has worked hard from a holistic perspective with an understanding of social norms to eradicate FC/FGM. Sustained efforts are being made at the local and community level towards eliminating FC/FGM (*ibid:* p. 17).

There are various countries in Africa where FC/FGM is practiced. These countries have made enormous efforts to abandon FC/FGM through education, enactment of laws, awareness campaigns, and conferences to eliminate the practice. The measures undertaken in the countries are listed below:

Burkina Faso: The Network for Human Rights and the Ministries of Justice, Defence and Security in Burkina Faso was supported by the Joint Programme to spread awareness among lawyers, judges and the police regarding the harmful consequences of FC/FGM. In 2011, five excisors and 57 accomplices were imprisoned for a period ranging from three months to three years for circumcising 30 girls. Ten cases of FC/FGM were also reported to the authorities through the toll-free anti-FC/FGM hotline (UNFPA and UNICEF 2012: p. 3).

While in 2011, 104 communities declared the elimination of FC/FGM. The Joint Programme also organised training to local advocates regarding human rights and women's rights, who campaign against FC/FGM in villages (*ibid:* p. 10).

Djibouti: In the year 2006, the prevalence of FC/FGM was 93 per cent. Three years of non-formal education was provided to 50 adults and 50 adolescents in 33 communities of Djibouti, which discussed various issues like literacy, human rights, democracy, conflict resolution, health, hygiene, and project management. After receiving education these groups shared their knowledge and experiences with friends, family, and within village as well as surrounding villages (*ibid:* p. 6).

They also took up community meetings regarding the harmful consequences of FC/FGM. A legal handbook was also printed for the officers of the justice system and the police in partnership with the National Commission of Human Rights (NCHR). The NCHR also dealt with gender-based violence, issues related to FC/FGM and answers regarding protection of women and children were mentioned. The handbook was also given to each district and to the city of Djibouti (*ibid:* p. 3).

On 3rd July 2011, there was a first public declaration regarding eradicating FC/FGM at national level, where representatives from 99 communities as well as officials from the national government and from bordering Punt land and Somali land met together in the capital city Djibouti (*ibid:* p. 6).

Eritrea: In 2011, four villages (each consists around 650 households and around 13,000 people) made a public declaration to eradicate FC/FGM in Eritrea. Moreover, 138 circumcisers publicly declared that they will stop performing FC/FGM on girls. Families have increasingly opposed the practice of FC/FGM and influenced the neighbours as well. Now, this practice is looked upon as shameful and with suspicious among people. There was also a 10-day training held regarding the HTP with the special focus on FC/FGM which gave rise to several anti-FC/FGM campaigns which was attended by local community leaders, members of the National Union of Eritrean Women, the National Union of Eritrea Youth and Students, village health committees, elderly people, religious leaders, traditional birth attendants and government officials. In addition, campaigns were also organised in schools and government offices which spread messages about the rights of women and girls, empowering them to protect themselves against FC/FGM and early marriages. Training also took place in five administrative regions to enhance action plans at community level to eradicate FC/FGM (*ibid:* pp. 9-10).

Egypt: In 2011, the historic political upheaval that started in Egypt and still continues has seriously shackled the judicial process. Due to this, cases on parents and doctors who were allegedly practicing FC/FGM were still pending. "medicalisation" of FC/FGM still continues to be a major problem in the country. Initiative has been taken by Joint Programme to urge the Ministry of Health to ban this practice and build up national laws against "medicalisation" of FC/FGM (*ibid:* p. 3). Due to the political issues there was a reduction in the number of eradication of FC/FGM from 5,143 to 3,602 among families. Still the initiatives by Joint Programme continued and spread awareness by working in more than 20 villages and 120 hamlets in Upper Egypt. Partnerships between Joint Programme and Child Protection Committees (CPC) were extended to 15 districts in four governorates in Upper Egypt to eradicate this practice. Short documentary film was also made at two locations in Upper Egypt with regard to the public declarations to eradicate FC/FGM in communities. This film was screened in other communities to encourage them to follow the same steps (*ibid:* p. 10).

Guinea: In Guinea *griots,* who are entertainers as well as educators, play a unique role in spreading messages regarding anti-FC/FGM. These *griots* with the support from Executive Office of the National Network of Traditional Communicators attend education sessions and enhance a culturally-sensitive plan of action and organise campaigns in their own communities to eradicate FC/FGM (UNFPA and UNICEF 2011: p. 13).

There is a booklet which contains laws regarding anti-FC/FGM which is provided to government officials and other partners. The National FC/FGM Action Plan has also been initiated and the Joint Programme works along with that towards strengthening the police to put forth law regarding anti-FC/FGM (UNFPA and UNICEF 2012: p. 3).

The Joint Programme also implements Community Empowerment Programme for training in human rights initiated by Tostan, a Senegal-based NGO. Due to the inter-village meetings, around 12,533 people were educated regarding the harmful consequences caused by this practice and led to 160 communities declaring the eradication of FC/FGM (*ibid:* p. 9).

Guinea-Bissau: The National Committee for the Abandonment of Harmful Practices works together closely with Guinea-Bissau's two main associations of Muslim leaders. This committee organises dialogue sessions with the religious leaders, with various Imams (leader of Muslim mosque or community), who discuss the issues regarding FC/FGM at the Friday sermons. Teachers in Quranic schools have also taken initiative to discuss about FC/FGM with their students. Both of these have played an important role in explaining to communities that FC/FGM is not part of Islam. Moreover, formally and, informally, leaders and royals have put in efforts to influence communities and convinced them against the practice (UNFPA and UNICEF 2011: pp. 12-13).

The country is moving towards developing better education, reproductive health, human rights and even improved economic opportunities to eradicate FC/FGM. The Joint Programme worked closely with the Ministry of Justice and the National Committee to Fight Harmful Practices (CNAPN) to organise three advocacy and information meetings on the draft of anti-FC/FGM law in Guinea-Bissau. After enormous efforts at the national level, on 5th July 2011, legislation approved criminalising of FC/FGM and the President signed it, and promulgated a law on the same day. This law has declared the practice of FC/FGM punishable by law and its violation includes imprisonment for five years (UNFPA and UNICEF 2012: p. 2).

Gambia: The traditional communicators in Gambia, work closely with health personnel to give information regarding FC/FGM at health clinics through dramas and songs in local languages. The Association for Promoting Girls and Women's Advancement with the support of UNFPA trains traditional communicators regarding anti-FC/FGM, as well as makes video materials to be used as a medium to spread awareness regarding eradication of FC/FGM (UNFPA and UNICEF 2011: p. 13).

The Joint Programme supported the National Steering Committee on FC/FGM in developing a National Plan of Action for the Accelerated Abandonment of FC/FGM. In the three eastern regions of Gambia, where there was high prevalence, Tostan's human-rights approach on community-level led to huge number of people eliminating this practice. On 12th June 2011, thousands of women, men, girls and boys from 105 villages were gathered at a sports stadium in the capital of the Upper River Region to make a joint public declaration to abandon FC/FGM as well as early and forced marriages. This declaration was highly publicised by media (UNFPA and UNICEF 2012: pp. 4, 8 and 9).

Kenya: In the Pokot community in Kenya, there is a high prevalence of FC/FGM. The school teachers in Kenya have put in great efforts towards eradicating FC/FGM. The NGO in Kenya named Women Empowerment Link (WEL) which is supported by the Joint Programme conducts training for primary teachers regarding anti-FC/FGM and trains them on how to deal with this matter with students as well as parents. After receiving training, these teachers organised workshops on FC/FGM and related topics namely, gender-based violence and human rights for parents, teachers and students aged 12-15 (as usually at this age girls are often cut). These workshops helped women in changing their minds to not cut their daughters. In 2011, the Pokot Council of Elders declared the eradication of FC/FGM. The meeting was organised by the Ministry of Gender, Children and Social Development where 3,000 people were part of this declaration. Similarly, another community also declared the eradication of FC/FGM which had a prevalence as high as 73 per cent, where 2,000 people were presented, while on the same day, a group of Chamus Morans (young men) publicly promised to marry uncut girls (*ibid:* pp. 11-12).

Mali: In 2011, a new Personal and Family Code, was adopted in Mali. This law states that "it forbids the impairment of a person's physical integrity, even in the context of a religious or traditional practice, when this is harmful to the person's health." In 2011, 21 villages of Mali grouped within of inter-marrying communities publicly declared the eradication of FC/FGM. Moreover, UNICEF supported capacity-building in three regions of Mali that had a high prevalence rates of FC/FGM. As a part of the capacity building initiative, 81,467 local and regional officials were educated about the harmful consequences of FC/FGM (*ibid:* pp. 4 and 8).

Mauritania: The second FC/FGM Action Plan was adopted by the National FC/FGM Committee and was implemented at the national level by the Ministry of Social Affairs, Children and the Family in Mauritania. The first time when Mauritania became a part of the Joint Programme, 5,355 people in the community declared the elimination of FC/FGM. And also during the information campaign regarding anti-FC/FGM held in 17 communities, 76.5 per cent of them supported the elimination of this practice (*ibid:* pp. 4 and 8).

Senegal: There has been an enormous progress towards eradicating FC/FGM in Senegal. This has been due to the work done by an organisation called Tostan which first started its human rights-based programme of community empowerment that led to the first declaration of FC/FGM eradication, in 1997. Due to this declaration, opposition against FC/FGM has moved at a fast pace. In 2011, 760 villages declared the eradication of FC/FGM and child marriage (*ibid*: p. 8).

Somalia: The prevalence of FC/FGM has been 98 per cent in Somalia, which is one of the highest in the world. The Joint Programme works with Swedish International Development Cooperation Agency (SIDA), and Australian Aid, in two autonomous regions of Somali land and Punt land to eradicate this practice (*ibid:* p. 6). In these two regions, two decrees outlawing all forms of FC/FGM were also drafted. The decree in Punt land was approved by the Cabinet but not by Parliament, as there were debates going on this issue. Some suggested that FC/FGM in its milder form "*Sunna*" should be continued. The Joint Programme is putting efforts and lobbying with the President through the Ministries and persuading them not to sign the present decree, but to wait until Parliament approves on a decree for eradicating FC/FGM (*ibid:* p. 4).

In 2011, the Joint Programme also supported 40 Child Protection Advocates (CPAs), who are members of the local community to work together in the CPCs and work towards eradicating violence against children, abuse and exploitation. They are also trained by the religious leaders that FC/FGM is not a part of Islam and do away with myths and convince that undergoing FC/FGM cannot maintain a girl's virginity or this practice does not make a girl "pure". After the training of these CPAs and through their awareness campaigns, 661 girls remained uncut as well as 12 girls who had gone through this practice were provided medical treatment and counselling due to serious consequences led by this practice (*ibid:* p. 4).

Moreover, the Joint Programme organised a dialogue where religious leaders, youth advocates, community "champions" who campaign to end FC/FGM, clan leaders, former circumcisers, and members of women's groups, Community Management Committees (CMCs), education committees and school-based Children's Rights clubs were trained in various fields such as advocacy, community mobilisation, and dialogue to de-link the practice from Islam, the dangers and consequences of FC/FGM and human rights. These people then took part actively in dialogue sessions, shared their experiences and worked together towards the eradication of this practice (*ibid:* p. 6).

Sudan: In Sudan, Saleema initiative works within the local culture, where they try to bring about change within the people without destroying their sense of dignity. This is done through their participation and decisions taken by them to abolish this practice after discussions are held on the harmful consequences faced by the girl post FC/FGM (UNFPA and UNICEF 2011: p. 11).

There are laws enacted to abolish FC/FGM, but they exist only in some states and not at the national level. In four states, Child Acts ban the practice, but only three States follow this act. The state named Southern Kordofan in Sudan has a special law against this practice (UNFPA and UNICEF 2012: p. 3).

Out of fifteen states thirteen states have launched programmes to eradicate the practice of FC/FGM, while five of states have launched these programmes since 2008. Education played a crucial role in changing the old tradition and beliefs. Various education programmes by three universities in community development are provided to illiterate women. After completing their graduation, seven hundred of these women were told about the harmful consequences of FC/FGM. This resulted in women's advocacy groups to campaign actively against this practice (*ibid:* p. 13).

Uganda: The practice of FC/FGM is practiced in a region mainly among two ethnic groups, the Sabiny and the Pokot in Uganda. "In recent years, the practice has been going underground, a trend likely related to the passage of Uganda's 2010 law against the practice". Most of the girls undergo FC/FGM in secret, they are taken far from villages without any traditional ceremonies and feast (*ibid:* p. 13).

In 2011, the Joint Programme along with its local partner organisations trained the local police and community monitors to put forth Uganda's law against FC/FGM, which was passed earlier in 2010. During early summer when girls are back from school, these monitors visit villages, interact with people around and talk to the families to check if FC/FGM continues, who is going to practice in the district as it is the tradition to perform FC/FGM on girls when they are back home for summer holidays. The programme gives monitors an air time on their mobile phones which helps them to inform police at district headquarters regarding the practice of FC/FGM (*ibid:* pp. 3-4).

Moreover in 2011, the Joint Programme also supported 70 community dialogues and 51 education sessions on FC/FGM, and issues like cultural identity and children's rights were discussed. About 317 numbers of girls in one district decided not to practice FC/FGM. Four hundred and thirty six uncut girls were honoured at the 16th Sabiny Culture Week, held in partnership with the Sabiny Elders Association, the Sabiny Athletics Association and the Uganda National Teachers Association (*ibid:* p. 13).

The Joint Programme funds a community organisation named Reproductive Educative and Community Health (REACH) in Uganda, which builds confidence among girls, where they share their experiences with each other as well as speak against FC/FGM to eradicate this practice. There was a meeting held at national level planning regarding FC/FGM by the Ministry of Gender, Labour and Social Development, where it was noticed that Christian churches played an important role in eradicating this practice (UNFPA and UNICEF 2011: p. 12). There have been various international NGOs that work at the regional level to help abandon this practice.

(c) Regional Efforts to Eradicate FC/FGM

The four international NGOs, who are the partners at sub-regional level, conduct various programmes and plan various policies to eradicate FC/FGM. These are:

> INTACT (The International Network to Analyse Communicate and Transform the Campaign against FC/FGM), an international NGO that consists of group of intellectuals, scholars who commit to bring about scientific reasons to eliminate FC/FGM and the Joint Programme also works with INTACT to abandon this practice. In 2010, INTACT started an online community to build up interaction and communication with people working on the Joint Programme in 17 countries to expand their network. It also conducts two online conferences in English and French, and works with leaders to eradicate FC/FGM. Moreover, they also have their quarterly e-newsletter which has current data regarding FC/FGM at the community and global level, the Joint Programme activities as well as their e-library updates Joint Programme communications and publications and uses Facebook to increase informal communication among their members. It also carries online discussion and web conferences held by FC/FGM experts, who are working with Joint programme. Further, it works towards abandoning "medicalisation" of FC/FGM by enacting laws which has led to increase in South-South communication, discussions, and sharing of experiences (UNFPA and UNICEF 2011: p. 21).

Other NGOs namely, Association for Women in Development (AIDOS) and No Peace Without Justice (NPWJ) are Italian-based organisations. AIDOS works in enhancing media strategies to eradicate the practice of FC/FGM with close ties with women's media organisations. The NPWJ follows the principles mentioned in the Maputo Protocol to the African Charter on Human and Peoples' Rights and on the Rights of Women in Africa to put forth laws against FC/FGM and encourages political commitment and move towards increase co-ordination and co-operation at international and sub-regional levels (UNFPA and UNICEF 2010: p. 11).

IAC is an NGO based in Addis Ababa. IAC works closely with religious leaders and young people to spread awareness on human rights, gender equality and respect for the bodily integrity of women and girls. AIDOS, NPWJ and IAC have also partnerships with NGOs at the national level, one of which is Tostan, Senegal-based NGO which is also a partner of the Joint Programme in six national programmes as well as collaborating on strategic planning at the global level (*ibid:* p. 11).

There are various NGOs in Ethiopia that are working intensively to eliminate FC/FGM. Their efforts on anti-FC/FGM initiatives are discussed in the section ahead.

Various Anti-FC/FGM NGOs in Ethiopia

Ethiopia is one of the African countries where FC/FGM is practiced. In the Afar region of Ethiopia, the prevalence rate of FC/FGM is very high. Due to increased awareness and spread of education as well as the Joint Programme's initiatives in the six districts of Afar region has led to reduction in the practice of FC/FGM. According to Rohi Weddu Pastoralist Women Development, a local organisation 4,000 girls have remained uncircumcised in the six districts of Afar region. There is an increased change in the mind-set of people and they are willingly ready to give up this practice after awareness and negative consequences faced by women and girls undergoing FC/FGM. One mother in the Afar region shared her feelings in a meeting held by Rohi Weddu. She says that:

> *I have one circumcised and two uncircumcised daughters. I did not circumcise the two younger girls after I got education from Rohi Weddu. Now we are seeing differences between the circumcised and un-circumcised girls. The uncircumcised girls are growing up healthy. Fewer girls are suffering from urine retention; fewer girls*

are dying from FC/FGM. We are hoping that when these girls become mothers, fewer of them will die due to FC/FGM (UNPPA and UNICEF 2011: p. 11).

Change in mind-set towards the practice of FC/FGM has led to the abandoning of FC/FGM in the year 2010, in two districts namely; Amibara and Awash Fentale of the Afar region (UNFPA and UNICEF 2011: p.11). Various NGOs working towards the abandonment of FC/FGM in Ethiopia are as follows:

Kembatta Mentii Gezzima—Tope (KMG): KMG is an NGO, founded in 1997 and located in Kembatta-Alaba-Tembaro Zone in the Southern Nations, Nationalities, Nations and People's Regional State (SNNPR) of Ethiopia. This NGO deals with the issues like "reproductive health, HIV/AIDS, FC/FGM, gender-based violence, civil and legal literacy as well as vocational training and livelihood programmes for women." KMG deals with FC/FGM from a point of view of gender issue as well as women's health and human rights (Kwaak and Schuringa 2006: p. 49).

This NGO works especially with younger generation, who become the role models for their friends and family around by opposing to the practice FC/FGM as well as getting married to an uncircumcised woman. A noteworthy incident happened in Kachebirra *Woreda* which was witnessed by over 2000 people. At a wedding, the bride wore a board saying that she was happy being uncircumcised as well as the groom wore a board saying that he was equally happy marrying an uncircumcised woman. This shows that awareness campaigns have brought a change towards eradicating the practice (*ibid*).

Hundee: Like KMG, Hundee is one of the indigenous NGO, founded in 1995, and it works in the five zones of Oromia region. The main aim of the Hundee is to work for the betterment of the marginalised communities as well as renew interest for its own community and raise it in all ways. It works in the fields of education centred on women's rights and harmful traditional practices (HTP). It also organises workshops on gender related issues and violence caused to women in form of FC/FGM, rape and abduction (*ibid:* pp. 49 and 50).

Afar Pastoralist Development Association (APDA)

APDA is a local Afar NGO-founded in 1993 and is managed by Afar nationals. It is located in four out of five zones of Afar. This NGO works in the domain of education as well as health issues of women. Moreover, it also works in the field of *Human Immunodeficiency Virus*/Acquired Immunodeficiency Syndrome (HIV/AIDS) and also gives education on HTPs such as FC/FGM (*ibid:* p. 50).

In 2003, APDA initiated efforts to eradicate FC/FGM as well as worked for women's rights in traditional marriages. It is also interesting to note that in APDA, there are women extension workers, who are literate Afar women. They are trained on the basis of an agreed curriculum using an APDA-written training manual. Their training is upgraded once a year and they are trained to change their mind-set regarding the harmful practices that prevails in the communities they belong to. These women focus on various issues like communities response on HIV/AIDS, hygiene and environmental sanitation, safer motherhood and care of young infants, response to traditional practices including FC/FGM, etc. The women extension workers also visit houses of families in the community and survey the problems faced by women and girls. They also teach basic education to women and children and help those who are in need of medical treatment.

APDA also made a film on the practice of FC/FGM which portrayed the procedure which scared the local community, as most of the time girls are circumcised alone rather in a group and most of them are unaware about the actual procedure undertaken on a girl. Moreover, APDA keeps a record of who has undergone FC/FGM, the girls who are about to undergo this practice are taken to religious leaders to do away the practice and if they refuse, they are imprisoned as FC/FGM is illegal in the Ethiopian

Constitution (Personal communication via e-mail dated 17 May 2012 from NGO, APDA (Afar region) Ethiopia).

Save the Children Norway-Ethiopia (SCN-E)

SCN-E is an organisation which is working for eradicating FC/FGM and other HTPs in Northern Gondar, Amhara region since long time. They have launched many projects regarding the rights of women and girls. Working since long period of time and gaining experience in Gondar, they have built up strategic partnership with various other organisations (Save the Children 2008: pp. 8 and 9).

The main work of this organisation is facilitating to others in form of technical, administrative, joint planning, and providing funds, receiving and compiling reports, ensuring quality assurance of documents, co-ordinating activities, and providing an environment of collaboration among the partners. And also SCN-E acts as an interface between the Embassy and the other partners (*ibid*).

CARE-Ethiopia

CARE is an organisation which has worked from the year 1996 in the Afar region with health-care agencies. In 2003, CARE—Awash FC/FGM Elimination Project was launched through gaining experience from a multi-country FC/FGM project which was held between 1999–2003, in that Afar region was also included in the project. This project focussed on health factor as well as eradicating FC/FGM. It also concentrated on other areas like women rights; HIV, health issues and improvement towards the community-based health-care system. CARE implemented project with close association with Afar regional authorities, including the local ministry Health and Women's Affairs Office, the Sheria Court and Islamic Affairs as well as village health committees, religious and community leaders. The other project in 2003-2006 financed by CARE-Norway and CARE-Austria was taken up in five different *Woredas* as well as at regional level. It gets funds from various organisations namely, CARE-Austria and CARE-Germany, as well as the Dutch Embassy and Farm Africa-Ethiopia. In addition, in

2007-2010 partnership-based project, Afar Women and Girls Sexual, Reproductive Health, and Livelihoods Rights Project was also carried out (*ibid:* pp. 10-11).

CARE's main aim is to give opportunity to community and people to take their own decision. It conducts discussions and debates, raise awareness campaigns at community level as well as communication with other villages regarding anti-FC/FGM and other HTPs. Other areas it works on is training birth attendants and primary health workers, spreads education to women and young mothers, spreads anti-FC/FGM messages through radio and also urge local governance for the betterment of women and girls health and livelihood security and set-up anti-FC/FGM committees at *Woreda* level (*ibid*).

Population Media Centre (PMC)

PMC is a non-profit, non-political, non-governmental and non-religious organisation started in Ethiopia in 2000. This organisation works through media that is radio, theatre, creative art as means to eradicate HTPs among them one of which is the practice of FC/FGM. Its project with SCN-E was from 2007-2010 (*ibid:* p. 12).

The aim of PMC project is to deal with women's and girl's issues regarding HTPs including FC/FGM. The project of PMC works at national level and also focusses on Afar and Somali regions. The anti-FC/FGM message is spread through radio, FM stations as well as serial drama, in vernacular languages on Radio Ethiopia. Special programmes are also organised for Afar and Somalia. Brochures, leaflets are also distributed as well as workshops and meetings held regarding anti-FC/FGM (*ibid*).

Ye Ethiopia Goji Limadawi Dirgitoch Aswogaj Maherber (EGLDAM)

The EGLDAM is an organisation that works for eradicating FC/FGM located in Addis Ababa. It is the national branch of IAC, a Pan-African organisation and has its own website and a documentation resource centre and regulates 40 NGOs. The EGLDAM partnership has been for two years (2007-2008). Its major work within the partnership of this organisation was to conduct surveys at the national level on HTPs which they took up in 1997 and later conducted in June 2008. The June 2008 survey marked remarkable changes at the level of prevalence, knowledge, attitude and intention as well as on behavioural change towards HTPs. Moreover, plans for future were also suggested (*ibid:* p. 13).

Other activity done by EGLDAM was the updating of a book named *"Old beyond Imaginings/Harmful Traditional Practices/Ethiopia"* based on 1997 survey in English as well as a translation in Amharic language (*ibid*).

Rohi-Weddu/Women's Affairs Bureau

Rohi-Weddu is a local NGO in Ethiopia started by people of Afar region. This NGO has a partnership with the Afar Women's Affairs Bureau. Their contract with SCN-E was from 2007-2009. These organisations have the same aims and objectives, i.e., the eradication of FG/FGM, but these two NGO's work in different zones. The Rohi-Weddu works in one and four zones (in all eleven *Woredas*), and Women's Affairs works in two and five (in all eight *Woredas*) (*ibid:* p. 14).

Rohi-Weddu also deals with issues like environment, livelihood, small-scale irrigation as well as income generating activities. It also aims to reduce the prevalence of FC/FGM. It also organises community dialogue with community leaders within the community regarding anti-FC/FGM (*ibid*).

Both the NGOs also organise radio-listening groups regarding anti-FC/FGM through Radio Fana and through Tigray radio that are provided to community leaders by the project organiser. It also registers birth records of girls for collecting information regarding girl's circumcision. The data states that seven hundred girls out of 3,000 have been registered as not circumcised. Meetings are also held at village levels to evaluate activities every quarterly. Officials at the regional level have also drafted a regional policy against the practice of FC/FGM. The most noteworthy development is that regional President had announced a day of mourning for the women and children, who had undergone suffering from such heinous practices, such as FC/FGM. There is also a Regional HTP committee where the issue of FC/FGM is emphasised, much more than the issue of HIV and AIDS. According to Rohi-Weddu, the mind-set of people is now changing and moving towards anti-FC/FGM (*ibid*).

These above NGOs have played vital role in empowering women and girls to abandon the practice of FC/FGM.

This chapter tries to understand that human rights guarantee moral rights all over the world. It also looks upon the issues of women's rights as human rights and thus raises a strong voice for their equal status.

Education and awareness play a vital role in changing the mind-set of people. The Joint Programme efforts led by UNFPA-UNICEF at community level have led to changes in the mind-set from within and to eradicate this practice through public pledges by the entire communities. This chapter has also highlighted the initiatives taken at national level taken by Joint Programme and local NGOs as well as by implementing laws in various countries. Moreover, the regional efforts by various NGOs namely, INTACT, AIDOS, NPWJ and IAC have also worked in a sustained way to bring this practice to an end with special focus on Ethiopia. It discusses the change towards the reduction in practice of FC/FGM in Ethiopia's Afar region where the practice is most prevalent. The efforts by Joint Programme and NGOs at the national and international levels are working at two levels, first through organising campaigns to educate against this heinous practice and bring about change from within, and second, to abandon this practice totally by arguing against this issue on the basis of human rights. The role of international organisations that are working towards eradication of FC/FGM is discussed in the subsequent chapter.

References

Deutsche GesellschaftfürInternationaleZusammenarbeit (GIZ) (Country Department Africa—Western Africa II, Angola and Pan-African Organisations and Programmes) (2011a) *Ending Female Genital Mutilation: Female Genital Mutilation and Legislation*, Germany: Deutsche Gesells chaftfür Internationale Zusammenar be it [Online], Available at:<http://www.giz.de/Themen/de/SID-29FF532C-C24431DD/dokumente/giz-fgm-EN-gesetzgebung-2011.pdf> (Accessed on 17/9/2012).

Deutsche GesellschaftfürInternationaleZusammenarbeit (GIZ) (Country Department Africa - Western Africa II, Angola and Pan-African Organisations and Programmes) (2011b) *Ending Female Genital Mutilation: Female Genital Mutilation and Human Rights*, Germany: Deutsche Gesell schaftfür Internationale Zusammenar be it [Online], Available at: <http://www.giz.de/Themen/de/SID-29FF532C-C24431DD/dokumente/giz-fgm-EN-menschenrechte-2011.pdf> (Accessed on 17/9/ 2012).

Office of the United Nations High Commissioner for Human Rights (2006), *Frequently Asked Questions on a Human Rights-based Approach to Development Cooperation*, New York and Geneva: United Nations [Online], Available at: <http://www.ohchr.org/Documents/Publications/FAQen.pdf>(Accessed on 30/12/ 2012).

Rahman, A. and Toubia, N. (2000) *Female Genital Mutilation: A Guide to Laws and Policies Worldwide*, London: Zed Books [Online], Available at: <http://books.google.co.in/books?hl=en&lr=&id=kEG6GaudxQEC&oi=fnd&pg=PR8&dq=history+of+female+genital+mutilation&ots=e74EjotccQ&sig=UD32rEFAdxnY6oWfu_UFqQVKGQ4#v=onepage&q=history%20of%20female%20genital%20mutilation&f=false>(Accessed on 19/6/ 2012).

Rwomire, A. (2001). *African Women and Children: Crisis and Response*, London: Praeger Publication.

Save the Children (2008). *Prevention and Eradication of Female Genital Mutilation (FGM) and Other Harmful Traditional Practices (HTPs) in Ethiopia*, Norway-Ethiopia and Partners. [Online], Available at:<https://docs.google.com/viewer?a=v&pid=gmail&attid=0.2& thid=1393e315d1e5c561 &mt=application/pdf&url=https://mail.google.com/mail/?ui%3D2%

26ik%3D595b2e0693% 26view%3Datt%26th%3D139 3e315d1e5c561%26attid%3D0. 2%26disp%3Dsafe%26r ealattid%3Df_h61wvjxh1%26zw&sig= AHIEtbQ OY1px0K5Ol tivbMgBblu3DaYVww>(Accessed on 19/8/ 2012).

Sehin, T. (2006). "Tackling Tradition: Examining Successful Strategies in the Mitigation of Female Genital Mutilation in Ethiopian Communities". In Kwaak, A. and Schuringa, M.W. *Gender, Society and Development Gender and Health: Policy and Practice: A Global Sourcebook*, Amsterdam: KIT (Royal Tropical Institute) and London: Oxfam GB, pp. 45-53 [Online], Available at: <http://www.kit.nl/net/KIT_Publicaties_output/ShowFile2.aspx?e=923>(Accessed on 15/6/2012).

UNFPA and UNICEF (2010). *The End is in Sight: Moving Toward The Abandonment of Female Genital Mutilation/ Cutting: Annual Report 2009.* New York: UNFPA [Online], Available at: <http://www.unfpa.org/webdav/site/global/shared/images/publications/2010/FGM-C%20Annual%20Report%202009_Eng.pdf> (Accessed on 16/8/2012).

UNFPA and UNICEF (2011). *UNFPA-UNICEF Joint Programme on Female Genital Mutilation-Cutting: Accelerating Change Annual Report 2010*, New York: UNFPA and UNICEF [Online], Available at: <http://www.unfpa.org/gender/docs/2010_Annual_Report_2.pdf>(Accessed on 16/8/2012).

UNFPA and UNICEF (2012).*UNFPA-UNICEF Joint Programme on Female Genital Mutilation-Cutting: Accelerating Change Annual Report 2011*, New York: UNFPA [Online], Available at: <http://www.unfpa.org/webdav/site/global/shared/documents/publications/2012/Annual_report_on_FGM-C_2011_low_res.pdf> (Accessed on 15/9/2012).

UNFPA (2012). *Promoting Gender Equality: Frequently Asked Questions about FGM/C*, UNFPA Available at: <http://www.unfpa.org/gender/practices2.htm>(Accessed on 17/10/2012).

UNFPA and Harvard School of Public Health (2010) *A Human Rights-Based Approach to Programming: Practical Information and Training Materials*, New York: UNFPA [Online], Available at: <http://www.unfpa.org/webdav/site/global/shared/documents/publications/2010/hrba/hrba_manual_in%20full.pdf> (Accessed on 30/12/2012).

WHO (2008). *Eliminating Female Genital Mutilation: An Interagency Statement OHCHR, UNAIDS, UNDP, UNECA, UNESCO, UNFPA, UNHCR, UNICEF, UNIFEM, WHO*, Switzerland: WHO [Online], Available at: <http://www.unfpa.org/webdav/site/global/shared/documents/publications/2008/eliminating_fgm.pdf>(Accessed on 14/7/2012).

WHO (2010). *Global Strategy to Stop Health-Care Providers from Performing Female Genital Mutilation UNAIDS, UNDP, UNFPA, UNHCR, UNICEF, UNIFEM, WHO, FIGO, ICN, IOM, MWIA, WCPT, WMA*, Switzerland: WHO [Online], Available at: <http://whqlibdoc.who.int/hq/2010/WHO_RHR_10.9_eng.pdf>(Accessed on 31/12/2012).

4 Role of International Organisations to Eradicate Female Circumcision/ Female Genital Mutilation in Africa

The Joint Programme, led by United Nations Population Fund (UNFPA) and United Nations Children's Fund (UNICEF) has played a major role in combating the practice of Female Circumcision/Female Genital Mutilation (FC/FGM) globally. International organisations and Non-governmental Organisations (NGOs) have played a major role in eradicating FC/FGM in Africa such as through efforts taken by the Joint Programme in Ethiopia and advocating pro-women, human rights based policies to end this heinous practice. The recent initiatives undertaken by the Joint Programme, and their policies at the global level have led to the decline of FC/ FGM in the countries where the programme is being implemented.

Since the 1990s, there has been a strong disapproval of FC/FGM at the global level. Various international organisations such as UNICEF (1979), UN General Assembly (1993), opposed the practice of FC/FGM. In 1997, UNICEF together with World Health Organisation (WHO) and UNFPA proposed the reduction in the prevalence of the practice over ten years and for the total abandonment of this practice within the next three generations. Similarly, the UN High Commissioner for Refugees (UNHCR) and the Office of the High Commissioner for Human Rights also disapproved this practice (Delaet 2009: pp. 405-406).

Moreover, various NGOs and other organisations like Reproductive Educative and Community Health (REACH), Amnesty International (AI), the International Commission of Jurists (ICJ), and the World Medical Association with their global agenda have also discouraged FC/FGM. Countries such as France, Switzerland, the United States (US), and many African countries have also enacted laws against FC/FGM as well as legal action taken against those that practices FC/FGM (*ibid:* p. 406). The persistent efforts of the Joint Programme in various African countries are discussed ahead.

Role of the Joint Programme in Africa

The two organisations UNFPA and UNICEF that were set-up in 2007, worked under national governments and encouraged community-based and national activities to bring about a positive social change towards eradicating FC/FGM. The Joint Programme aimed to work together with the initiatives taken up earlier at the country and regional level through their programmes rather than in isolation. The Joint Programme worked in partnership with governments, civil society, religious leaders, communities and key stakeholders. The goal of the Programme was to gain 40 per cent reduction in the practice of FC/FGM on infants and girls up to age 15 as well as to free at least one country from this practice by 2012 (UNFPA and UNICEF 2011 p.1). In addition, UNFPA and UNICEF through their Programme expect to reduce the practice of FC/FGM by 40 per cent in 16 countries by the year 2015 (UNFPA 2007: p.10).

The collaborative efforts led by the Joint Programme have played a pivotal role in eradicating FC/FGM at the national as well as at the global level since mid-1980s. In the year 2008, the Programme was carried out in eight countries namely, Djibouti, Ethiopia, Egypt, Guinea, Guinea-Bissau, Kenya, Senegal, Sudan and gradually included few more countries such as Burkina Faso, Eritrea, Gambia, Ghana, Mali, Mauritania, Somalia, Tanzania and Uganda and covered up to 17 countries. The UNFPA and UNICEF headquarters first consultation with the eight countries regarding the Joint Programme took place in Florence, Italy, which was based on the grounds of common understanding which is noted in Programme document. The technical assistance and policy guidance to these countries was located in the UNFPA headquarters in New York. There were positive results reported from countries like Djibouti, Ethiopia, Guinea, Guinea Bissau and Kenya, where governments supported the launch of the Joint Programme. "In Djibouti and Guinea, the First Ladies officially launched the Joint Programme, while Ministers in charge of children and gender officially launched the Joint Programme in Guinea Bissau and Kenya. In Ethiopia, the regional vice-president launched the Joint Programme" (UNFPA and UNICEF 2009: p. 4).

There have been enormous changes in the year 2009 towards the eradication of FC/FGM. The main emphasis of the Programme was to raise the partnerships with government authorities at local as well as at the national level, with religious authorities and local religious leaders, the media, civil society organisations of women and in the arena of education and health. The partnerships also helped in spreading knowledge, empowering communities and creating an environment to bring about social change and collectively work towards eradicating FC/FGM. The Programme also focussed on the betterment of reproductive health of girls and women who have undergone FC/FGM (UNFPA and UNICEF 2010).

The Joint Programme started working with the WHO on an inter-regional initiative in sub-Saharan Africa and Arab nations to make sure that the medical profession strictly opposed the practice of FC/FGM. The "medicalisation" of FC/FGM has been a serious issue and has been observed in six countries covered by the Programme. Various strategies are put forth to strengthen the physician's code of ethics namely "Do no harm" (*ibid*).

In 2009, at the global level, the Programme drafted the UN Secretary General's report on the Girl Child which particularly focussed on the practice of FC/FGM. The equivalent to Secretary General's Report was the UN General Assembly Resolution on the Girl Child in 2009 which encouraged the national organisations, civil society and communities to prevent the rights of girls and women and move towards eradicating FC/FGM (*ibid*).

There have been various aims and objectives put forth by the Joint Programme to eliminate the practice of FC/FGM that are listed below:

The Aims and Objectives of the Joint Programme to Eradicate FC/FGM

The Joint Programme had a detailed set of tasks to abandon FC/FGM. These are as follows:

- *Effective enactment and enforcement of legislation against FC/FGM.*
- *Knowledge dissemination of socio-cultural dynamics of FC/FGM practice.*
- *Collaboration with key development partners on a common framework for the abandonment of FC/FGM.*
- *Evidence-based data for programming and policies.*
- *Consolidation of existing partnerships and forging of new partnerships.*
- *Expanding network of religious leaders advocating abandonment of FC/FGM.*
- *Media campaigns emphasising FC/FGM abandonment process in sub-Saharan Africa, Egypt and Sudan.*
- *Better integration of implications of FC/FGM practice into reproductive health strategies.*
- *Building donor support to pool resources for a global movement towards abandonment of FC/FGM* (UNFPA and UNICEF 2009: p. 11).

The Joint Programme is using the above strategies as tool to eradicate FC/FGM. Further the key efforts done by the Programme within the year 2010-11 are discussed ahead.

A Note on the Efforts Taken by the Joint Programme (2010-2011)

There have been progressive results achieved by the Joint Programme by 2010. This was possible due to the sustained efforts of the Programme. The initiative has also increased its capacities by backing new research, enforcing laws to abandon FC/FGM. Along with that it also worked with the media, community, religious networks and the health sector on several issues. The Programme has also persistently worked in increasing the understanding of the social norms that surrounds the practice of FC/FGM within countries and of the cross-border and global level policies that affects it (UNFPA and UNICEF 2011a: p. 2).

During 2010, the Joint Programme has also worked jointly with many key development partners and supported eight global advocacy events on FC/FGM at the global level. It also provided technical assistance to the Ministerial meeting on FC/FGM, co-chaired by the governments of Egypt and Italy as an official side-event to the UN General Assembly. The main objective of this meeting was to discuss the issue regarding the potentiality of tabling a UN resolution on FC/FGM at the General Assembly. The outcome of this meeting was that the UN member states recognised the practice of FC/FGM as a social norm and agreed to take steps and measures for eradicating FC/FGM by spreading education as well as working towards enforcing laws which needed help from the community to transform the social norms that are more gender sensitive (*ibid:* p. 25).

At the time of the 2010 Commission on the Status of Women (CSW), the programme supported an official side event on FC/FGM that was called upon by governments of Egypt, Italy and the African group which was chaired by the First lady of Burkina Faso. This event helped in guiding policy for the Convention on the Elimination of All Forms of Discrimination Against Women (CEDAW), and Convention on the Rights of the Child (CRC) in choosing the focus areas regarding harmful practice and gender-based violence as the subjects for the first joint general comment and recommendation in 2010 (*ibid*).

There has been progress in the work of the Joint Programme's efforts towards eradicating FC/FGM. They have been supporting capacity-building for raising awareness regarding the social norms perspective to UN agency staff, national governments and other partners. The staff members of UNFPA and UNICEF attended a two-week course on the practical application of social norms research, organised in partnership with the University of Pennsylvania. After this course, one of the participant carried out training on FC/FGM for members of the government, police and NGOs in Ouagadougou, the capital city of Burkina Faso. While many of the participants urged for similar course at the country level (*ibid)*.

Various new partnerships were introduced by the Joint Programme, such as with support from Luxembourg. Further, it also joined hands with the cabinet of European Commissioner named Designate Viviane Reding through meeting which led to future cooperation towards the advancement of a joint European strategy on FC/FGM for the eradication of this practice in Africa and other Diaspora communities (*ibid)*.

Similarly, the Joint Programme also reinforced its partnerships with many UN agencies, international co-operation and development agencies and private foundations. Due to such partnerships it garners support and helps pool resources for a global movement for eradicating this practice (*ibid*).

During September 2011, the Steering Committee of the Joint Programme agreed to expand the Programme till 31st December 2013. This was done due to more positive results gained within countries and at the global level. It was also considered that the expansion would enhance the possibility to pool in more resources and use these resources for efficient results. Thus, the Steering Committee will have better chances to finish the evaluation of the programme before its termination, which will enable it to accomplish feedback and application of lessons (UNFPA and UNICEF 2012: p. 31). There have been various policies laid by the Joint Programme to eliminate FC/FGM that are discussed ahead.

Various Policies to Eradicate FC/FGM

The Joint Programme has continued its support to provide technical guidance regarding the content of a proposed UN General Assembly Resolution by directing towards more commitment and action by UN Member States to end this practice.

There have been various initiatives and steps put forth to combat FC/FGM. These are as follows:

- At the time of the African Union Assembly, 17th Ordinary Session, held from 30 June to 1st July 2011, the African Union (AU) recommended tabling the resolution. Following various discussion and meetings, it was concluded by the governments to postpone the resolution up to the 67th Session of the General Assembly in October 2012. The reason behind the delay was to improve the text and attain the support of additional Member States. UNFPA and UNICEF have agreed to continue and provide technical assistance to Member States as they move ahead in the preparation of the resolution (UNFPA and UNICEF 2012: p. 31).
- At the time of the 55th session of the CSW held in February 2011, UNFPA and UNICEF took part in a high-level side-event on FC/FGM organised by the governments of Burkina Faso, Egypt and Italy. About more than 100 activists, government and media representatives were present at this meeting. Moreover, the involved agencies prepared a report on its current programmatic work and accomplishments, based on the social norms perspective and the holistic, human rights-based approach (*ibid*).
- The 2012 Secretary-General's Report on 'Ending Female Genital Mutilation' was prepared for the 56th session of the CSW. This report mentions that measures have been taken by UN Member States and activities held within the United Nations (UN) system to deal with the issue of FC/FGM, in accordance to resolution 54/7 of the CSW. Further, it sheds light on the numerous efforts of the Joint Programme in the fields of law-making, building

policies, assisting community-based efforts and developing evidence-base work on eradicating FC/FGM. The concluding part of the report focusses on certain issues such as disseminating human rights-based approach in all the communities, establishing partnership and including several stakeholders at different stages of the Programme. It also recommends this approach which has been encouraged by the Joint Programme and at the same time uplifting the persistent challenges faced regarding the limited resources (UNFPA and UNICEF 2011b: pp. 2-3).

- February 6, 2011 was celebrated as an International Zero Tolerance Day to FC/FGM where UNFPA Executive Director Babatunde Osotimehin and UNICEF Executive Director Anthony Lake, passed a joint statement to revive their engagement to abandon the practice of FC/FGM. This message was also spread widely through press releases and the social media. They stated:

  We call on the global community to join us in this critical effort. Together, we can abolish FC/FGM in one generation and help millions of girls and women to live healthier, fuller lives (*ibid*: p. 3).

- In addition, the Joint Programme also provided technical assistance to the CEDAW and CRC Committees for the advancement of the Joint/General/Recommendation on harmful practices (*ibid:* p. 3).

- Persistent efforts regarding the high level advocacy and meetings led to debates about FC/FGM in the House of Commons of the United Kingdom (UK) Parliament (*ibid*).

- Moreover, UNFPA and UNICEF also provided technical assistance to the World Health Assembly report A64/26 on FC/FGM, which reported on the implementation of recommendations accompanied with World Assembly Resolution WHA 61.16. Further, the report also provided data regarding the activities of the Joint Programme, and the development towards understanding the continuation of FC/FGM in Africa as a social norm (UNFPA and UNICEF 2012: p. 31).

Through the above measures there have been various policies drawn to reduce FC/FGM. The following section studies the efforts undertaken by the Joint Programme in the subsequent and more recent years.

In the year 2011, there have been increasing efforts of the Joint Programme to have an impact on global and national policies related to the abandonment of FC/FGM. During October 2011, there was a three-day international conference on Research, Health-care and Preventive Measures for FC/FGM and the Strengthening of Leadership and Research in Africa, organised by UNFPA, WHO and other partners. It was attended by various participants from countries namely, Australia, Ethiopia, Ghana, Indonesia, Kenya, Mali, Norway, Sudan, USA, and others. This conference examined the existing knowledge base and gaps therein regarding the adverse health effects of FC/FGM, and its treatment, and evaluating the efficiency of community-based interventions in response to the practice FC/FGM. The next aim of this conference was to recognise various methods of reinforcing leadership and to generate good quality research on FC/FGM in Africa. This was done through developing a network that linked researchers in Africa. It also investigated the potentiality of setting up an African centre for research and leadership training for eradicating FC/FGM. Eventually, it discussed various recommendations regarding programming on FC/FGM, and focussing on mainstreaming FC/FGM work into health programmes. Besides, it also recommended that the research related to FC/FGM "Centre of Excellence" be set-up in Nairobi, where UNFPA is working towards setting up the centre (*ibid*: p. 32).

In 2011, through its progressive efforts, the UNFPA and UNICEF were involved in reviewing the Joint Programme's structure for reviewing the outcomes. This was conducted in co-operation with Harvard University's Programme on Health and Human Rights, whose scholars carried out adequate literature review of the human rights-based approach (HRBA), and its relation to FC/FGM and culture. The data was assembled from the country offices in 2010. Next year in 2011, the reviewed structure emphasised on the human rights perspective of the Programme, and its relation towards the practice of FC/FGM and concentrated on cultural respect. The Joint Programme also started working together with country offices to structure the programme that is suitable to local realties and the existing Monitoring and Evaluation (M and E) systems. UNFPA held a meeting in Gambia to strengthen country-level capacity on M and E and the Logical Framework Approach (log-frame). Moreover, two internet-based meetings took place in the last quarter of 2011 to consult with country offices regarding the process of operationalising the reviewed log-frame into the recent M and E systems. Ultimately, the Programme equipped the country offices with a specific furnished Excel database that included the indicators of the reviewed structure which makes it easier to track and update data on FC/FGM that would further help assess the Joint Programme's activities for 2012 via country office annual reports (*ibid*).

During 2011, the annual meeting of the Joint Programme countries took place with sub-groups of countries in Dakar, and Nairobi to increase discussions and mutual learning, which enhances capacity-building. There were representatives from the 15 countries, regional offices and headquarters that came together in March 2011 to exchange their views and experiences and improve annual work plans for the year. Every country that attended the meeting had produced a report on their progress, three years earlier, in the year 2010 (*ibid*).

Further the Joint Programme distributed about 200 copies of Innocenti Research Centre's publication named,

'Dynamics of Social Change towards the Abandonment of FC/FGM in Five African countries' as well as the link to about 300 development partners such as NGOs, governments and UN agencies. This publication expresses the achievements made by the national policies that assisted community-based activities actions in Joint Programme countries namely, Egypt, Ethiopia, Kenya, Senegal and Sudan (*ibid*).

Through the entire period of 2011, the Joint Programme continued its efforts by spreading knowledge and awareness about the social norms perspective to agency staff, national governments and partners. During July, UNICEF organised a second two-week training programme, 'Learning Course on Advances in Social Norms' in collaboration with the University of Pennsylvania, a leader in this field. This course provided 49 UNICEF colleagues from country offices, most of them were UNICEF's focal points on FC/FGM, new analytical devices to direct situations of violence (including FC/FGM), abuse and exploitation of children, as well as those characterised by stigma and discrimination were also developed (*ibid:* p. 33).

Besides in March 2011, comprehensive technical aid was provided to the Uganda team as well as a one-day interactive orientation was organised on the subject of social norms for members of the UNICEF and UNFPA Uganda country office staff and partners, including staff from government, other UN agencies and NGOs. The orientation overlaid basic concepts of social norms theory, including the role of beliefs and expectations and the significance of harmonising change among groups that practice harmful norms. Likewise, UNICEF Guinea also organised a similar kind of training on social norms that was conducted by the Burkina Faso staff office, who had taken part in this course at the University of Pennsylvania (*ibid*).

In the 2010 report, it is mentioned that the Joint Programme in co-operation with academic and NGO partners advanced the study conducted by the UNICEF to investigate the role of value-based education in achieving successive social transformations. The beginning of the research was held in Senegal in early 2010 that spelt out the facts that encourage positive debates regarding discriminatory practices such as FC/FGM and how these practices get eradicated. By 2011, the analysis was conducted and an introductory report was discussed with UNICEF. The researchers listed several supplementary questions that needed additional interviews and field research (*ibid*).

Moreover, UNFPA moved towards the expansion of a training manual on including social norms theory and related concepts into programming steps towards the eradication of FC/FGM. The making of the manual namely, 2008 'Interagency Statement for the Elimination of Female Genital Mutilation', will be presented to the NGO managers and government officials the achievement gained due to programming on FC/FGM that have promoted the eradication of this practice (*ibid:* p. 33). There were also certain barriers that surfaced during the implementation of the Joint Programme's efforts towards eliminating FC/FGM.

Problems Faced During the Eradication of FC/FGM

With the ongoing implementation by the Joint Programme at the country level, during 2011 it came across various obstacles related to the abandoning of FC/FGM, while dealing with several key leaders and communities. The various problems faced by the Joint Programme during the process for eradicating FC/FGM are as follows:

- First, the global financial crisis widely affected the budget from the government and other donors to fulfill new promises. On the other hand, the country level capacity had been raised due to success of the programmes at the local level. Country offices have paid more attention towards raising funds that fulfill the objectives of the Joint Programme, but still the problems have remained unsolved and budgets do not meet the requirements in implementing the programme.

- Second, there has been a scaling down in the anti-FC/FGM work undertaken by the Joint Programme. This was due to the political tensions that took place in Egypt in the aftermath of Hosni Mubarak's fall from power. The former first lady Suzanne Mubarak was involved in the eradication of this practice. The close connection of Ms Mubarak's with the anti-FC/FGM movement has led to the decline of the Joint Programmes' anti-FC/FGM initiatives. The reason for the decline was the strong opposition against eradicating of FC/FGM from conservative, pro-FC/FGM forces as well as reformers, who strongly wanted to do shift Egypt from Hosni Mubarak's anti-FC/FGM policies.
- Besides, from among the fifteen member countries of the Joint Programme, some of the conservative forces have opposed the anti-FC/FGM initiatives. The supporters of FC/FGM differ from religious leaders and convey their views and state that cutting is an obligation; of their religion, towards family member and at the same time necessary for a girl to become a woman. For example, in Guinea people supported this practice by spreading rumours around the country that uncut girls would suffer with fatal sickness, if they were not cut and it may lead to their death. Many of them have supported this practice because they believe that anti-FC/FGM steps reflect cultural imperialism inflicted by the Western world on Africa on their indigenous culture, and that they should not be pressurised to change their age-old systems.
- Further, the Joint Programme has been structured in such a way where all countries benefit from a comprehensive mix of programme strategies towards the eradication of FC/FGM. Though, these strategies have worked towards the betterment of the women in the region, at times the Programme failed to connect with religious leaders or organising media

campaigns, which is essential for a sustained policy for the eradication of FC/FGM.

- Finally, they have also come across difficulties in reviewing the M and E framework. This is due to the lack of data regarding the association between FC/ FGM and reproductive health problem. The Programme is working towards updating this data and shortly this data will be updated. Moreover, the demographic data by Demographic and Health Surveys (DHS), and Multiple Indicator Cluster Surveys (MICS) that is available for 2005 is due for updating shortly and will be of immense help in the policy planning in the years ahead (UNFPA and UNICEF 2012: pp. 35-36).

Instead of numerous problem faced by the Joint Programme, their efforts were sustained and did not go in vain. The increased efforts by the Joint Programme in Ethiopia, and its positive and encouraging outcomes are discussed in the subsequent sections of this chapter.

Efforts of UNFPA and UNICEF in Ethiopia to Eradicate FC/FGM

There are several proposed programmes and projects initiated by UNFPA and UNICEF in Ethiopia which are as follows:

In 1998, 'UNFPA proposed programmes and projects' focussed especially towards the reproductive health issue namely, maternal and child health, adolescent reproductive health, reproductive tract infections including HIV and Acquired Immuno Deficiency Syndrome (AIDS), family planning, and harmful traditional practices (HTP) such as early marriage and FC/FGM. These issues would be forwarded in all activities hold up by the programme and would be given more preferences (UNFPA 1998: p. 7).

The 2006, 'UNFPA: Country Programme for Ethiopia' focussed on securing the rights of women's and girl's in the field of gender-based violence, reproductive health, family planning, FC/FGM and HIV/AIDS. This can be achieved by supporting community-based programmes to spread education regarding reproductive rights and women's empowerment; and also making them aware of their own rights and supporting them to take their own decisions to end such violence faced by them (UNFPA 2006: p. 5).

The 2011, 'UNICEF: Draft country programme document: Ethiopia' highlighted on moving towards eradicating HTPs, particularly FC/FGM and early marriage (UNICEF 2011: p. 3).There have been positive changes in spreading knowledge about the HTPs and lessening such practices in Ethiopia. The 2005, the Demographic and Health Survey states that 81 per cent of women aged 45-49 years were circumcised, which has declined up to 63 per cent among young women, aged 15-19 years (*ibid*: p. 4).

There has been immense progress towards combating FC/FGM in Ethiopia. In the Afar region, in two districts namely, Burimodaytu and Argoba, which consist of 28 sub-districts (more than 200 communities-villages) and comprise a total population of 53,515 (Burimodaytu (31,786) and Argoba (21,729)) an official call for eradicating of FC/FGM was made on the 10th and 12th January, 2012. Regional government officials, religious leaders, elders, clan leaders and thousands of people were a part of this anti-FC/FGM declaration (UNFPA and UNICEF 2011: p. 5).

Future Plans towards Eradicating FC/FGM

Creative efforts of the Joint Programme function in two ways. These are; first by creating a programmatic content and second, through partnerships with other organisations. The year 2012 was the Joint Programme's fifth year of implementation. After five years it became essential to examine the progress towards the eradication of FC/FGM in various countries led by the Joint Programme. This would be examined jointly by the Evaluation Offices of both agencies to assure that an independent and credible exercise has been taken place. The evaluators will report the future global and national efforts to further their efforts on the eradication of FC/FGM. Future plans will be structured and taken into account the past global and country-level evaluations of FC/FGM related activities (UNFPA and UNICEF 2012: p. 39).

It is important to note that an evaluation enables to safeguard accountability to donors and other stakeholders. More specifically, it also helps in producing knowledge and understanding of the subject. It also recognises certain good practices about field experiences and adopts the best ones and put into practice. Further, it weighs the achievements and coherence of the Joint Programme's innovative, holistic and multi-sectoral approach to accelerate the eradication of FC/FGM and recommends policies and programmes regarding anti-FC/FGM measures for the future. At last, it looked upon UNICEF and UNFPA's successes and challenges while carrying out the Programme and 'Delivering as One UN' (*ibid*).

The Joint Programme set various targets to be achieved during the year 2012. These included; intensifying capacity-building for partner organisations, making it possible to efficiently conduct evidenced-based community interventions; capacity development and advocacy activities with medical professional associations (mid-wives, Obstetrics and Gynaecology (OBGYN), doctors, etc., to assure that they stop medicalising the practice of FC/FGM and actively be a part to eradicate this abhorrent practice. As FC/FGM leads to harmful consequences on health and affects the mental and physical well-being, thus this issue has been included into sexual and reproductive health programmes, raising capacity with law enforcement agents to enact laws against FC/FGM, increasing webinars on M and E and use of revised indicators in programme of M and E activities to develop better evidence-base for interventions, encourage sub-regional collaboration, and assure that eradication of FC/FGM takes place on a sub-regional and regional level. The Programme also encouraged the upholding of public commitments to eradicate this practice and continued their efforts to make sure that the communities abandon this practice permanently (*ibid).*

The Joint Programme has worked persistently to produce more efficient global commitment by Member States to abandon FC/FGM. It expects that the future UN General Assembly Resolutions will continue its efforts to eradicate FC/FGM world-wide. Pursuant to this objective, the December 2011, Secretary-General's report on 'Ending Female Genital Mutilation' stated:

> *Despite the increase in efforts and focus on the abandonment of female genital mutilation, the prevalence of the practice remains a cause for concern. The challenges that have been identified include insufficient enforcement of legislation and policies; limited resource allocated for their implementation; insufficient monitoring and evaluation of the impact of laws, policies and programmes; and lack of data to facilitate monitoring of progress (ibid).*

These above plans and strategies of the Joint Programme to abandon the practice of FC/FGM in the years ahead may lead to success and result in the elimination of this practice in its entirety.

This chapter studies the work done by Joint Programme in the countries of Africa where FC/FGM is being practiced. It further discusses the manner in which the Joint Programme implements various activities such as enforcing laws by working in cooperation with the government, media, communities and religious leaders. It also highlights that the Programme provided technical assistance as well as build partnerships with NGOs and other organisation and UN General Assembly to end to this practice.

Further the Joint Programme also provided technical support and policy guidance to CRC and CEDAW Committees to eradicate this practice. It has also played a major role in the Secretary General's Report on 'Girl Child' in 'Ending Female Genital Mutilation' by encouraging national governments, civil society and communities to prevent the rights of girls and women's as well as passing laws, building policies to eradicate this practice. Further, it also highlights the ongoing efforts by the Joint Programme that are implemented in partnership with communities, government, religious leaders, and other community-based organisations rather than in isolation. This has changed the mind-set of people to some extent and social reform has been taken place among the communities that are now convinced of the need to abandon FC/FGM. The programme has also worked in updating M and E system for improved data based on FC/FGM related issues. This chapter has a specific focus on Ethiopia and discusses the various policies and plans, led by Joint Programme that has encouraged many communities and villages to give up with this practice. Throughout the Joint Programme implementation plan since five years, i.e., since 2008, despite the hurdles in their work against FC/FGM, the Programme has worked persistently to achieve their goal of eliminating the deplorable practice of FC/FGM.

The concluding section will further summarise the major findings of this research on FC/FGM and the various initiatives taken towards eradicating this inhuman practice.

References

Delaet, Debra L. (2009). 'Framing Male circumcision as a Human Rights issue? Contributions to the Debate Over the Universality of Human Rights', *Journal of Human Rights,* Vol. 8(4). London and New York: Taylor and Francis pp. 405-426 [Online], Available at: <http://web.ebscohost.com/ehost/detail?vid=4&hid=105&sid=37b45c05-0c0948fca9dd191f6e4d%40sessionmgr110&bdata=JnNpdGU9ZWhvc3QtbGl2ZQ%3d%3d#db=aph&AN=45141170>(Accessed on 20/10/2012).

UNFPA (1998). *United Nations Population Fund Proposed Projects and Programmes* [Online], Available at: <http://ethiopia.unfpa.org/drive/eth9801.pdf (Accessed on 27/5/2012).

UNFPA (2006). *United Nations Population Fund: Country Programme for Ethiopia* [Online], Available at: <http://ethiopia.unfpa.org/drive/dpfpa_eth_6_eng.pdf>(Accessed on 27/5/2012).

UNFPA (2007). *A Holistic Approach to Abandonment of Female Genital Mutilation/Cutting,* New York: UNFPA [Online], Available at: <http://www.unfpa.org/webdav/site/global/shared/documents/publications/2007/726_filename_fgm.pdf> (Accessed on 12/4/2012).

UNFPA and UNICEF (2009). *UNFPA-UNICEF Joint Programme on Female Genital Mutilation/ Cutting: Accelerating Change 2008, Annual Report,* New York: UNFPA [Online], Available at:<http://www.unfpa.org/webdav/site/global/shared/images/publications/2009/FGM-C%20Annual%20Report%202008.pdf> (Accessed on 16/7/ 2012).

UNFPA and UNICEF (2010). *The End Is In Sight: Moving Toward The Abandonment of Female Genital Mutilation/ Cutting: Annual Report 2009.* New York: UNFPA [Online], Available at:<http://www.unfpa.org/webdav/site/global/shared/images/publications/2010/FGM-C%20Annual%20Report%202009_Eng.pdf> (Accessed on 16/8/ 2012).

UNFPA and UNICEF (2011a). *UNFPA-UNICEF Joint Programme on Female genital Mutilation-Cutting: Accelerating Change Annual Report 2010,* New York: UNFPA and UNICEF [Online], Available at:<http://www.unfpa.org/gender/docs/2010_Annual_Report_2.pdf>(Accessed on 16/8/ 2012).

UNFPA and UNICEF (2011b). *UNFPA-UNICEF Joint Programme for the Acceleration of the Abandonment of FGM/C: Key Results and Highlights 2011,* New York: UNFPA and UNICEF [Online], Available at: <http://www.unfpa.org/webdav/site/global/shared/documents/publications/2012/Annual_Report_2011.pdf>(Accessed on 16/11/ 2012).

UNFPA and UNICEF (2012). *UNFPA-UNICEF Joint Programme on Female Genital Mutilation-Cutting: Accelerating Change Annual Report 2011,* New York: UNFPA [Online], Available at: <http://www.unfpa.org/webdav/site/global/shared/documents/publications/2012/Annual_report_on_FGM-C_2011_low_res.pdf>(Accessed on 15/9/2012).

UNICEF (2011). *Draft Country Programme Document: Ethiopia* [Online], Available at: [Online] Available at: <http://www.unicef.org/about/execboard/files/2011-PL8—Ethiopia—HR-JIL-CW—12APR11—FINAL.pdf>(Accessed on 27/5/ 2012).

Conclusion

The practice of FC/FGM is a social norm which enforces women and girls to undergo circumcision of their genitals. It is an inhuman and painful practice due to the societal pressures from within a community in several countries in Africa. Therefore, it is of essence that we understand the causes and the harmful consequences of FC/FGM from within the framework of human rights violation. The technological advances like "medicalisation" of FC/FGM have provided new tools for the continuation of this practice, and it has become even more difficult to uproot it. One of the major findings of this work is that there is a direct correlation between the advancement of education and the decline in the practice of FC/FGM in countries of Africa. Statistical data indicates that if the mother is educated, she is turn spreads awareness about the undesirability of FC/FGM and encourages her daughters to further spread consciousness among the future generations of women.

In Ethiopia, patriarchy is deeply entrenched, and women have a subordinate position due to their gender specific socialisation. Women themselves perpetrate FC/FGM through reinforcing the practice on their own daughters and other women and justify it on grounds of tradition, culture or upholding the existing social norms. There have been sharp differences in the urban and rural attitudes towards the practice of FC/FGM. Personal communication with an Ethiopian official in Mumbai in 2012, revealed that in the urban cities, the practice of FC/FGM is on the wane due to education and the broad mind-set, though in the rural areas, high illiteracy is a major impediment to the eradication of FC/FGM. According to Africa watchers though a steady progress is being made in the direction of eliminating FC/FGM, but the complete eradication of FC/FGM will take several more years and efforts are ongoing to change the mindset of people.

The statistical data in Chapter II of this book describes the attitudes of people towards the practice of FC/FGM and efforts undertaken towards its eradication in Ethiopia and more specifically in the Afar region of the country where FC/FGM has the highest rate of prevalence. The most important fact worth noting is that the percentage of mother's, who decide to mutilate their daughter is higher as compared to the percentage of father's who decide to mutilate their daughters. This shows that women themselves want the other girls/women to practice FC/FGM and thus carry forward the entrenched tradition and continue to be a part of the community.

There are cases of women in Ethiopia, who continue to believe that undergoing FC/FGM will ensure virginity which is a precondition for marriage and for getting a suitable husband because some men refuse to marry women who are not circumcised. On the other hand, it is interesting to note the cases of women who have been victims of FC/FGM are now combating the practice of FC/FGM through the efforts of local NGOs and other international organisation such as WHO, UNFPA, UNICEF and others, via their intensive awareness campaigns.

The 20th century brought about various documented efforts to eradicate FC/FGM from a human rights perspective as detailed in Chapter III of this book. There have been positive changes towards the abandonment of FC/FGM at the national level in several countries of Africa namely, Burkina Faso, Djibouti, Egypt, Eritrea, Ethiopia, Guinea-Bissau, Guinea, Gambia, Kenya, Mali, Mauritania, Somalia, Sudan, Senegal and Uganda have made progress towards the eradication of FC/FGM due to the support from the UN programmes as well as national and international NGOs. Several communities in Burkina Faso, Egypt, Gambia and Sudan, amongst others have publicly declared their anti-FGM stance and given up the practice of FC/FGM completely.

The Joint Programme has worked persistently since mid-1980s to abandon FC/FGM at the national as well as the global level. Successes in countries like Djibouti, Ethiopia, Guinea, Guinea Bissau and Kenya are noticeable as governments of these countries have actively supported the launch of the Joint Programme. The year 2010 also brought about better opportunities and positivity to end this practice. Due to the continuous efforts by the Joint programme more innovative ways were initiated to abandon this practice. Efforts throughout 2011 have been directed towards disseminating knowledge and awareness about the social norms regarding anti-FC/FGM to the UN agency staff, national governments and partners that have accelerated the anti-FC/FGM campaign. These significant endeavours have helped reduce the practice to a limited extent.

In Ethiopia, UNFPA and UNICEF's joint initiatives have focussed on women's issues such as reproductive health, rights of women and girls, harmful traditional practices, including FC/FGM. In 2012, in the Afar region of Ethiopia, two districts namely, Burimodaytu and Argoba officially abandoned FC/FGM. This shows that the Joint Programme's efforts and spread of education have contributed immensely in the eradication of FC/FGM to some extent in Ethiopia (UNFPA and UNICEF 2011b: p. 5).

In the year 2012, the high-level side event at the 67 Session of the UN General Assembly reaffirmed an increased commitment towards raising awareness about the evil practice of FC/FGM and planned actions among many partners to eradicate FC/FGM. The event was hosted by Madame Chantal Boni Yay, First Lady of Benin, and Madame Chantal Campaore, the First Lady of Burkina Faso, where UNFPA Executive Director Babatunde Osotimehin; Ms. Emma Bonino, Vice President of the Italian Senate; and representatives from UNICEF and UN Women were also present. All of them came to the consensus that there is a need for a concerted global partnership between governments, civil society, NGO, academia and relevant UN agencies to end FC/FGM in its entirety (UNFPA 2012a).

At the above referred event, the UNFPA director Dr. Osotimehin expressed: "The resolution to end FC/FGM has to be owned by African countries. The communities have to embrace it" (*ibid).*

Therefore, raising awareness through education and other means is crucial to changing the mind-sets and the eradication of FC/FGM. For example, there have been vast changes noticed in various countries of Africa such as in Mali where farmers in remote villages listen to radio talks shows related to debates on FC/FGM. In Senegal, community groups speak about FC/FGM from the perspective of human rights and a course on FC/FGM and its harmful consequences have been included in the national education curriculum. While in Somalia, the Islamic preachers disapproved of this practice on television and media. In the Horn of Africa, in Eritrea, posters on the roadside have unequivocally opposed the practice of FC/FGM. In the eastern part of the continent, in Kenya, policemen trained in human rights are working towards imposing new laws to abandon FC/FGM practice while in Uganda and Somalia in the same region 'Rescue' missions are carried out by community activists to prevent girls from undergoing cutting. In Sudan, through the organisation Saleema, multi-media campaigns have been launched to educate women and girls and enable them to change their attitudes and encourage them to abandon FC/FGM. From Gambia to Ethiopia, former circumcisers are giving up their profession and denouncing FC/FGM in public declarations (UNFPA 2012d). These cases show that there has been a slow but gradual movement towards the abandonment of FC/FGM in several countries in Africa.

Through awareness campaigns and increased voices of religious leaders who have confirmed that FC/FGM does not have a religious sanction, changes have occurred in the mind-set of people, and they are encouraged to abandon the barbaric practice of FC/FGM. Thus, due to sustained efforts, there is a decline in the prevalence of FC/FGM in many countries of Africa in general and to a limited extent in Ethiopia, though national and international NGO's are working towards a zero prevalence rate of FC/FGM, commensurate with the prevailing human rights norms of the 21st century.

However, to achieve the goal of a FC/FGM free continent, a more determined effort needs to be waged. As case studies in this book highlight, it is heartening to note that social norms are shifting and moving towards eradicating FC/FGM. Thus, it can be stated emphatically that education is the game changer. The increase in awareness through education and advocacy has played a crucial role in changing the mind-sets of women and girls, who have been practicing and supporting FC/FGM. These efforts aim to persuade girls and women and solicit their support in spreading the anti-FC/FGM message collectively and eradicate the inhuman practice from the face of this earth.

As Babatunde Osotimehin rightly states, "it is truly heartening that social norms and cultural practices are changing and communities are uniting to protect the rights of their girls and women" (UNFPA 2012c). The UNICEF Executive Director Anthony Lake, on an optimistic note stated that progress shows that it is possible to end FC/FGM. He further states, "FC/FGM is not only deeply wrong, we can and must end it to help millions of girls and women lead healthier lives" (UNFPA 2013).

Initiative taken at an individual level may lead to the elimination of the practice of FC/FGM, and the beginning has to be made within one's family. This in turn will have a ripple effect on the immediate community and the awareness will spread beyond the family, even if gradually. Anti-FC/FGM activists are hopeful that an increase in the level of awareness through education and advocacy launched by national and international organisations will lead to the eradication of FC/FGM in Ethiopia as well as other countries where the archaic and barbaric practice continues to prevail.

References

UNFPA (2012a). *Using the Opportunity of the General Assembly to Speak Out Against FGM/C,* UNFPA [Online], Available at: <http://www.unfpa.org/public/cache/offonce/home/news/pid/12159;jsessionid=93014334AABFC9275207C79995F98973.jahia01> (Accessed on 20/12/2012).

UNFPA (2012c). *Executive Director, Angelique Kidjo Call for an End to* UNFPA [Online], Available at: <http://www.unfpa.org/public/home/news/pid/10140>(Accessed on 11/9/ 2012).

UNFPA (2012d). *Tide is Turning Against Female Genital Mutilation/Cutting,* UNFPA [Online], Available at:<http://www.unfpa.org/public/home/news/pid/10799> (Accessed on 26/10/ 2012).

UNFPA (2013). *Fewer Girls Threatened by Female Genital Mutilation: UNFPA and UNICEF call for accelerated efforts as the practice begins to decline,* UNFPA [Online], Available at:<http://www.unfpa.org/public/cache/offonce/home/news/pid/12684>(Accessed on 8/ 2/2013).

UNFPA and UNICEF (2011b) *UNFPA-UNICEF Joint Programme for the Acceleration of the Abandonment of FGM/C: Key Results and Highlights 2011,* New York: UNFPA and UNICEF [Online], Available at: <http://www.unfpa.org/webdav/site/global/shared/documents/publications/2012/Annual_Report_2011.pdf> (Accessed on 16/11/2012).

Bibliography

Primary Sources

CNN (20th November 2012), Reporter Isha Sesay 'U.N. director: 'Women will Change the World', [Online], Available at:<http://edition.cnn.com/2012/11/20/world/africa/babatunde-osotimehin-unfpa-women/index.html> (Accessed on 6/1/2013).

CNN (30th November 2012), Reporter Nima Elbagir 'Give African Women a Voice, say Activists', [Online], Available at:<http://edition.cnn.com/2012/11/30/world/africa/africa-womens-decade-rights/index.html?iid=article_sidebar> (Accessed on 6/1/2013).

BBC News (18th April 2012). 'Swedish Minister in 'Racist Cake' Controversy', [Online], Available at:<http://www.bbc.com/news/world-europe-17749533> (Accessed on 7/6/2012).

Ethiopian Society of Population studies (2008), *Gender Inequality and Women's Empowerment: In-depth Analysis of the Ethiopian Demographic and Health Survey 2005*, Addis Ababa: UNFPA [Online], Available at:<http://ethiopia.unfpa.org/drive/Gender.pdf> (Accessed on 17/5/ 2012).

Gelaw, A. (2010). *Abandoning Female Genital Cutting/Mutilation in the Afar Region of Ethiopia,* UNFPA [Online], Available at: <http://www.unfpa.org/public/news/pid/5141> (Accessed on 22/4/2012).

Gelaw, A. (2012). *Two More Corners of Ethiopia Call for an End to Genital Cutting,* UNFPA [Online], Available at: <http://www.unfpa.org/public/home/news/pid/9964>(Accessed on 22/4/2012).

Getachew, I. (2006). *Battling an Ancient Tradition: Female*

Genital Mutilation in Ethiopia, UNICEF [Online], Available at: <http://www.unicef.org/infobycountry/ethiopia_34881.html>(Accessed on 22/4/2012).

Kembatta Women's Self-Help Center (2006). *Whole Body Healthy Life 2006: Freedom from Female Genital Excision (FGE),* Addis Ababa: Ethiopia. [Online], Available at: <https://docs.google.com/viewer?a=v&pid=gmail&attid=0.1&thid=1393e315d1e5c561&mt=application/pdf&url=https://mail.google.com/mail/?ui%3D2%26ik%3D595b2e0693%26view%3Datt%26th%3D1393e315d1e5c561%26attid%3D0.1%26disp%3Dsafe%26realattid%3Df_h61wt8cf0%26zw&sig=AHIEtbRPC7RSqezo9WkI7md4O23SL6f1xQ>(Accessed on 19/8/2012).

Save the Children (2008). *Prevention and Eradication of Female Genital Mutilation (FGM) and Other Harmful Traditional Practices (HTPs) in Ethiopia,* Norway-Ethiopia and Partners. [Online], Available at:<https://docs.google.com/viewer?a=v&pid=gmail&attid=0.2&thid=1393e315d1e5c561&mt=application/pdf&url=https://mail.google.com/mail/?ui%3D2%26ik%3D595b2e0693%26view%3Datt%26th%3D1393e315d1e5c561%26attid%3D0.2%26disp%3Dsafe%26realattid%3Df_h61wvjxh1%26zw&sig=AHIEtbQOY1px0K5OltivbMgBblu3DaYVww>(Accessed on 19/8/2012).

Tulloch, T. (2009). *In Ethiopia, African Women Parliamentarians Condemn Female Genital Mutilation,* UNICEF [Online], Available at: <http://www.unicef.org/infobycountry/ethiopia_51122.html>(Accessed on 22/4/2012).

UNFPA (1998). *United Nations Population Fund Proposed Projects and Programmes* [Online], Available at: <http://ethiopia.unfpa.org/drive/eth9801.pdf>(Accessed on 27/5/2012).

UNFPA (2006). *United Nations Population Fund: Country Programme for Ethiopia* [Online] Available at: <http://ethiopia.unfpa.org/drive/dpfpa_eth_6_eng.pdf>(Accessed on 27/5/2012).

UNFPA (2007). *A Holistic Approach to Abandonment of Female Genital Mutilation/Cutting,* New York: UNFPA [Online], Available at: <http://www.unfpa.org/webdav/site/global/shared/documents/publications/2007/726_filename_fgm.pdf>(Accessed on 12/4/2012).

UNFPA and Harvard School of Public Health (2010). *A Human Rights-Based Approach to Programming: Practical Information and Training Materials*, New York: UNFPA [Online], Available at: <http://www.unfpa.org/webdav/site/global/shared/documents/publications/2010/hrba/hrba_manual_in%20full.pdf>(Accessed on 30/12/2012).

UNFPA and Population Council (2010). *Ethiopia Young Adult Survey: A Study in Seven Regions,* New York: UNFPA [Online], Available at: <http://ethiopia.unfpa.org/drive/EthiopianYoungAdultSurvey2010.pdf> (Accessed on 12/6/2012).

UNFPA and UNICEF (2009). *UNFPA-UNICEF Joint Programme on Female Genital Mutilation/Cutting: Accelerating Change 2008 Annual Report*, New York: UNFPA [Online], Available at: <http://www.unfpa.org/webdav/site/global/shared/images/publications/2009/FGM-C%20Annual%20Report%202008.pdf> (Accessed on 16/7/2012).

UNFPA and UNICEF (2010). *The End Is In Sight: Moving Toward the Abandonment of Female Genital Mutilation/Cutting: Annual Report 2009*. New York: UNFPA [Online], Available at: <http://www.unfpa.org/webdav/site/global/shared/images/publications/2010/FGM-C%20Annual%20Report%202009_Eng.pdf> (Accessed on 16/8/2012).

UNFPA and UNICEF (2011a). *UNFPA-UNICEF Joint Programme on Female Genital Mutilation-Cutting: Accelerating Change Annual Report 2010*, New York: UNFPA and UNICEF [Online], Available at:<http://www.unfpa.org/gender/docs/2010_Annual_Report_2.pdf>(Accessed on 16/8/2012).

UNFPA and UNICEF (2011b). *UNFPA-UNICEF Joint Programme for the Acceleration of the Abandonment of FGM/C: Key Results and Highlights 2011*, New York: UNFPA and UNICEF [Online], Available at: <http://www.unfpa.org/webdav/site/global/shared/documents/publications/2012/Annual_Report_2011.pdf> (Accessed on 16/11/2012).

UNFPA and UNICEF (2012) *UNFPA-UNICEF Joint Programmme on Female Genital Mutilation-Cutting: Accelerating Change Annual Report 2011*, New York: UNFPA [Online], Available at: <http://www.unfpa.org/webdav/site/global/shared/documents/publications/2012/Annual_report_on_FGM-C_2011_ low_res.pdf> (Accessed on 15/9/2012).

UNFPA (2012). *Two Districts in Afar Region Declare Abandonment of FGM/*C,UNFPA [Online], Available at: <http://ethiopia.unfpa.org/2012/01/24/4476/two_districts_in_afar_region_declare_abandonment_of_fgm_c/>(Accessed on 22/4/2012).

UNFPA (2012). *Promoting Gender Equality: Frequently Asked Questions about FGM/C*, UNFPA [Online], Available at: <http://www.unfpa.org/gender/practices2.htm> (Accessed on 17/10/2012).

UNFPA (2012a). *Using the Opportunity of the General Assembly to Speak Out Against FGM/C*, UNFPA [Online], Available at: <http://www.unfpa.org/public/cache/offonce/home/news/pid/12159;jsessionid=93014334AABFC9275207C79995F98973.jahia01>(Accessed on 20/12/2012).

UNFPA (2012b). *'Cultural Tradition' is No Excuse for Female Genital Mutilation/ Cutting*, UNFPA [Online], Available at:<https://www.unfpa.org/public/home/news/pid/10080>(Accessed on 11/9/2012).

UNFPA (2012c). *Executive Director, Angelique Kidjo Call for an End to* UNFPA [Online], Available at: <http://www.unfpa.org/public/home/news/pid/10140> (Accessed on 11/9/2012).

UNFPA (2012d). *Tide is Turning against Female Genital Mutilation/ Cutting*, UNFPA [Online], Available at:<http:/ / www.unfpa.org/ public / home / news / pid / 10799>(Accessed on 26/10/2012).

UNFPA (2013). *Fewer Girls Threatened by Female Genital Mutilation: UNFPA and UNICEF call for accelerated efforts as the practice begins to decline*, UNFPA [Online], Available at: <http: / /www.unfpa.org/ public / cache / offonce / home/ news / pid / 12684>(Accessed on 8/2/2013).

UNFPA (2014). *International Day of Zero Tolerance for Female Genital Mutilation: Statement of Dr. Babatunde Osotimehin, Executive Director, UNFPA, the United Nations Population Fund*, UNFPA[Online], Available at: <http: / / www.unfpa.org/ public / home / news / pid / 16602> (Accessed on 10/2/2014).

UNICEF (2011). *Draft Country Programme Document: Ethiopia* [Online] Available at: [Online], Available at: <http: / / www.unicef.org/ about / execboard / files / 2011-PL8—Ethiopia—HR-JIL-CW—12APR11—FINAL.pdf> (Accessed on 27/5/2012).

UNICEF (2011). *Two Districts in Northern Ethiopia Declare an End to Female Genital Cutting*, UNICEF [Online], Available at:<http: / /www.unicef.org/ infobycountry/ ethiopia_57521. html>(Accessed on 22/4/2012).

UNICEF(2013). *Female Genital Mutilation/ Cutting: A Statistical Overview and Exploration of the Dynamics of Change*, New York: UNICEF [Online], Available at: <http:/ /www.childinfo.org/ files / FGMC_Low_Sept2013.pdf> (Accessed on 18/10/ 2013).

WHO (2001). *Female Genital Mutilation: Integrating the Prevention and the Management of the Health Complications into the Curricula of Nursing and Midwifery: A Teacher's Guide*, Geneva: WHO, [Online], Available at:<http: / / www.who.int/ gender / other_health / teachersguide. pdf>(Accessed on 14/4/2012).

WHO (2008). *Eliminating Female Genital Mutilation: An*

Interagency Statement OHCHR, UNAIDS, UNDP, UNECA, UNESCO, UNFPA, UNHCR, UNICEF, UNIFEM, WHO, Switzerland: WHO [Online], Available at:<http://www.unfpa.org/webdav/site/global/shared/documents/publications/2008/eliminating_fgm.pdf> (Accessed on 14/7/2012).

WHO (2010). *Global Strategy to Stop Health-care Providers from Performing Female Genital Mutilation UNAIDS, UNDP, UNFPA, UNHCR, UNICEF, UNIFEM, WHO, FIGO, ICN, IOM, MWIA, WCPT, WMA*, Switzerland: WHO [Online], Available at: <http://whqlibdoc.who.int/hq/2010/WHO_RHR_10.9_eng.pdf>(Accessed on 31/12/2012).

WHO (2012). *International Day of Zero Tolerance to Female Genital Mutilation*, WHO [Online], Available at: <http://www.who.int/mediacentre/events/annual/femalegenitalmutilation/en/index.html>(Accessed on 15/9/2012).

WHO (2012). *Sexual and Reproductive Health: Female Genital Mutilation and Other Harmful Practice,* WHO [Online], Available at:<http://www.who.int/reproductivehealth/topics/fgm/prevalence/en/index.html>(Accessed on 13/6/2012).

Women's UN Report Network (WUNRN) (2012). 'FGM – Female Genital Mutilation—Women and Girls, UN Commission on the Status of Women' CSW 56, New York, Available at: [Online], Available at: <www.wunrn.com/powerpoint/2012/FGM_12_csw.pps>(Accessed on 16/10/2012).

Yoder, P.S., Abderrahim N., and Zhuzhuni A. (2004). *Female Genital Cutting in the Demographic Health Surveys: A Critical and Comparative Analysis*, Calverton: ORC Marco. (DHS Comparative Reports No. 7).

Secondary Sources

Books

Dubois, Nicole (2003) *Socio-cognitive Approach to Social Norms*, London and New York: Routledge Taylor and

Francis [Online], Available at:<http://books.google.co.in/books?hl=en&lr=&id=7C3idYDvBW4C&oi=fnd&pg=PP1&dq=books+on+social+norms+&ots=OJnw9E7zf7&sig=giko5R7SeFbXIvasEjQYKZjg_I#v=onepage&q=books%20on%20social%20norms&f=false>(Accessed on 30/12/2012).

Leslie, M.O. (1994). *Recreating Ourselves: African Women and Critical Transformations,* New Jersey: Africa World Press Inc.

Momoh, Comfort (2005). *Female Genital Mutilation,* Oxon: Radcliffe Publishing [Online], Available at:<http://books.google.co.in/books?id=dVjIP0RfV AMC&printsec=frontcover&dq=comfort+momoh&hl=en&sa=X&ei=6H90T_jqO4jirAe385HQDQ&ved=0CDIQ6AEwAA#v=onepage&q=comfort%20momoh&f=false>(Accessed on 23/7/2012).

Office of the United Nations High Commissioner for Human Rights (2006). *Frequently Asked Questions on a Human Rights-Based Approach to Development Cooperation,* New York and Geneva: United Nations [Online], Available at:<http://www.ohchr.org/Documents/Publications/FAQen.pdf> (Accessed on 30/12/ 2012).

Rwomire, A. (2001). *African Women and Children: Crisis and Response,* London: Praeger Publication.

Rahman, A. and Toubia, N. (2000). *Female Genital Mutilation: A Guide to Laws and Policies Worldwide,* London: Zed Books [Online], Available at: <http://books.google.co.in/books?hl=en&lr=&id=kEG6GaudxQEC&oi=fnd&pg=PR8&dq=history+of+female+genital+mutilation&ots=e74EjotccQ&sig=UD32rEFAdxnY6oWfu_UFqQVKGQ4#v=onepage&q=history%20of%20female%20genital%20mutilation&f=false>(Accessed on 19/6/2012).

Sehin, T. (2006). "Tackling Tradition: Examining Successful Strategies in the Mitigation of Female Genital Mutilation in Ethiopian Communities". In Kwaak, A. and Schuringa, M.W. *Gender, Society and Development Gender and Health: Policy and Practice: A Global Sourcebook,*

Amsterdam: KIT (Royal Tropical Institute) and London: Oxfam GB, pp.45-53 [Online], Available at:<http://www.kit.nl/net/KIT_Publicaties_output/ShowFile2.aspx?e=923>(Accessed on 15/6/2012).

Online Journals and Articles

Beatrice, S. and Pamela N. (1998). 'Campaigning against Female Genital Mutilation in Ethiopia Using Popular Education', *Gender and Development,* Vol. 6, (2), USA: Taylor and Francis pp. 44-52 [Online], Available at:<http://www.jstor.org/stable/4030344>(Accessed on 20/5/2012).

Deutsche Gesellschaftfür Internationale Zusammenarbeit (GIZ) (Country Department Africa - Western Africa II, Angola and Pan-African Organisations and Programmes) (2011a) *Ending Female Genital Mutilation:Female Genital Mutilation and Legislation*, Germany: Deutsche Gesellschaftfür InternationaleZusammenarbeit[Online], Available at:<http://www.giz.de/Themen/de/SID-29FF532C-C24431DD/dokumente/giz-fgm-EN-gesetzgebung-2011.pdf>(Accessed on 17/9/2012).

Deutsche GesellschaftfürInternationaleZusammenarbeit (GIZ) (Country Department Africa - Western Africa II, Angola and Pan-African Organisations and Programmes) (2011b) *Ending Female Genital Mutilation: Female Genital Mutilation and Human Rights*, Germany: Deutsche Gesell schaftfür Internationale Zusammenarbeit [Online], Available at: <http://www.giz.de/Themen/de/SID-29FF532C-C24431DD/dokumente/giz-fgm-EN-menschenrechte-2011.pdf> (Accessed on 17/9/2012).

Delaet, Debra L. (2009) 'Framing Male circumcision as a Human Rights issue? Contributions to the Debate Over the Universality of Human Rights', *Journal of Human Rights,* Vol. 8(4), London and New York: Taylor and Francis, pp. 405-426 [Online], Available at: <http://web.ebscohost.com/ehost/detail?vid=4&hid=105&sid=37b45c05-0c0948fca9dd191f6e4d%40sessionmgr110&bdata=Jn

NpdGU9ZWhvc3QtbGl2ZQ%3d%3d#db=aph&AN=45141170> (Accessed on 20/10/ 2012).

Douglas and *et al.* (2003). 'Ethiopia: African Women Meet to Oppose Genital Mutilation', *News Africa*, Vol. 33 (3-4), Washington: Off Our Backs, p. 4 [Online], Available at:<http://web.ebscohost.com/ehost/pdfviewer/pdfviewer?vid=5&hid=8&sid=80cef024-b566-47b0-b06d-d80796e06aee%40sessionmgr13>(Accessed on 20/5/ 2012).

Gebre, B. (2007). 'Ending Female Genital Mutilation in Ethiopia', *The Lancet*, Vol. 369 (9579) p. 2071 [Online], Available at: <http://www.lancet.com/journals/lancet/article/PIIS0140-6736(07)60964-7/fulltext> (Accessed on 22/4/ 2012).

Mitike, G. and Deressa, W. (2009). 'Prevalence and Associated Factors of Female Genital Mutilation among Somali refugees in Eastern Ethiopia: A Cross-Sectional Study', *BMC Public Health*, Addis Ababa: School of Public Health, Vol. 9, pp. 264-273 [Online], Available at:<http://web.ebscohost.com/ehost/pdfviewer/pdfviewer?vid=4&hid=11&sid=80cef024-b566-47b0-b06d-d80796e06aee%40sessionmgr13>(Accessed on 20/5/ 2012).

Missailidis, K. and Medhin- Gebre, M. (2000). 'Female Genital Mutilation in Eastern Ethiopia', *Lancet*, Vol. 356 (9224), Uppsala: Department of Women's and Children's Health, International Child Health, p.137 [Online], Available at:<http://web.ebscohost.com/ehost/pdfviewer/pdfviewer?vid=4&hid=8&sid=80cef024-b566-47b0-b06d-d80796e06aee%40sessionmgr13>(Accessed on 20/5/ 2012).

Thein, M. (1995) *Female Genital Mutilation and the Risk of HIV*, SARA Issues Paper, Washington: Academy for Educational Development, pp. 1-12.

Index